Technical Writing Exam

About Peterson's

Peterson's® has been your trusted educational publisher for more than 50 years. It's a milestone we're quite proud of, as we continue to offer the most accurate, dependable, high-quality educational content in the field, providing you with everything you need to succeed. No matter where you are on your academic or professional path, you can rely on Peterson's for our books, online information, expert test-prep tools, the most up-to-date education exploration data, and the highest quality career success resources—everything you need to achieve your education goals. For our complete line of products, visit **www.petersons.com.**

For more information, contact Peterson's, 4380 S. Syracuse Street, Suite 200, Denver CO 80237; 800-338-3282 Ext. 54229; or find us online at **www.petersons.com**.

ISBN: 978-0-7689-4474-7

Printed in the United States of America

10 9 8 7 6 5 4 3 2 1   23 22 21

Contents

Before You Begin

HOW THIS BOOK IS ORGANIZED

Peterson's *Master the*™ *DSST*® *Technical Writing Exam* provides a diagnostic test, subject-matter review, and a post-test.

- **Diagnostic Test**—Twenty multiple-choice questions, followed by an answer key with detailed answer explanations
- **Assessment Grid**—A chart designed to help you identify areas that you need to focus on based on your test results
- **Subject-Matter Review**—General overview of the exam subject, followed by a review of the relevant topics and terminology covered on the exam
- **Post-test**—Sixty multiple-choice questions, followed by an answer key and detailed answer explanations

The purpose of the diagnostic test is to help you figure out what you know—or don't know. The twenty multiple-choice questions are similar to the ones found on the DSST exam, and they should provide you with a good idea of what to expect. Once you take the diagnostic test, check your answers to see how you did. Included with each correct answer is a brief explanation regarding why a specific answer is correct, and in many cases, why other options are incorrect. Use the assessment grid to identify the questions you miss so that you can spend more time reviewing that information later. As with any exam, knowing your weak spots greatly improves your chances of success.

Following the diagnostic test is a subject-matter review. The review summarizes the various topics covered on the DSST exam. Key terms are defined; important concepts are explained; and when appropriate, examples are provided. As you read the review, some of the information may seem familiar while other information may seem foreign. Again, take note of the unfamiliar because that will most likely cause you problems on the actual exam.

After studying the subject-matter review, you should be ready for the post-test. The post-test contains sixty multiple-choice items, and it will serve as a dry run for the real DSST exam. There are complete answer explanations at the end of the test.

OTHER DSST® PRODUCTS BY PETERSON'S

Books, flashcards, practice tests, and videos available online at www.petersons.com/testprep/dsst

- A History of the Vietnam War
- Art of the Western World
- Astronomy
- Business Mathematics
- Business Ethics and Society
- Civil War and Reconstruction
- Computing and Information Technology
- Criminal Justice
- Environmental Science
- Ethics in America
- Ethics in Technology
- Foundations of Education
- Fundamentals of College Algebra
- Fundamentals of Counseling
- Fundamentals of Cybersecurity
- General Anthropology
- Health and Human Development
- History of the Soviet Union
- Human Resource Management
- Introduction to Business
- Introduction to Geography
- Introduction to Geology
- Introduction to Law Enforcement
- Introduction to World Religions
- Lifespan Developmental Psychology
- Math for Liberal Arts
- Management Information Systems
- Money and Banking
- Organizational Behavior
- Personal Finance
- Principles of Advanced English Composition
- Principles of Finance
- Principles of Public Speaking
- Principles of Statistics
- Principles of Supervision
- Substance Abuse
- Technical Writing

Like what you see? Get unlimited access to Peterson's full catalog of DSST practice tests, instructional videos, flashcards, and more for **75% off the first month!** Go to **www.petersons.com/testprep/dsst** and use coupon code **DSST2020** at checkout. Offer expires July 1, 2021.

Chapter 1

All About the DSST® Exam

WHAT IS DSST®?

Previously known as the DANTES Subject Standardized Tests, the DSST program provides the opportunity for individuals to earn college credit for what they have learned outside of the traditional classroom. Accepted or administered at more than 1,900 colleges and universities nationwide and approved by the American Council on Education (ACE), the DSST program enables individuals to use the knowledge they have acquired outside the classroom to accomplish their educational and professional goals.

WHY TAKE A DSST® EXAM?

DSST exams offer a way for you to save both time and money in your quest for a college education. Why enroll in a college course in a subject you already understand? For more than 30 years, the DSST program has offered the perfect solution for individuals who are knowledgeable in a specific subject and want to save both time and money. A passing score on a DSST exam provides physical evidence to universities of proficiency in a specific subject. More than 1,900 accredited and respected colleges and universities across the nation award undergraduate credit for passing scores on DSST exams. With the DSST program, individuals can shave months off the time it takes to earn a degree.

The DSST program offers numerous advantages for individuals in all stages of their educational development:

- Adult learners
- College students
- Military personnel

Adult learners desiring college degrees face unique circumstances—demanding work schedules, family responsibilities, and tight budgets. Yet adult learners also have years of valuable work experience that can frequently be applied toward a degree through the DSST program. For example, adult learners with on-the-job experience in business and management might be able to skip the Business 101 courses if they earn passing marks on DSST exams such as Introduction to Business and Principles of Supervision.

Adult learners can put their prior learning into action and move forward with more advanced course work. Adults who have never enrolled in a college course may feel a little uncertain about their abilities. If this describes your situation, then sign up for a DSST exam and see how you do. A passing score may be the boost you need to realize your dream of earning a degree. With family and work commitments, adult learners often feel they lack the time to attend college. The DSST program provides adult learners with the unique opportunity to work toward college degrees without the time constraints of semester-long course work. DSST exams take two hours or less to complete. In one weekend, you could earn credit for multiple college courses.

The DSST exams also benefit students who are already enrolled in a college or university. With college tuition costs on the rise, most students face financial challenges. The fee for each DSST exam starts at $85 (plus administration fees charged by some testing facilities)—significantly less than the $750 average cost of a 3-hour college class. Maximize tuition assistance by taking DSST exams for introductory or mandatory course work. Once you earn a passing score on a DSST exam, you are free to move on to higher-level course work in that subject matter, take desired electives, or focus on courses in a chosen major.

Not only do college students and adult learners profit from DSST exams, but military personnel reap the benefits as well. If you are a member of the armed services at home or abroad, you can initiate your post-military career by taking DSST exams in areas with which you have experience. Military personnel can gain credit anywhere in the world, thanks to the fact that almost all of the tests are available through the internet at designated testing locations. DSST testing facilities are located at more than 500 military installations, so service members on active duty can get a jump-start on a post-military career with the DSST program. As an additional incentive, DANTES (Defense Activity for Non-Traditional Education Support) provides funding for DSST test fees for eligible members of the military.

More than 30 subject-matter tests are available in the fields of Business, Humanities, Math, Physical Science, Social Sciences, and Technology.

Available DSST® Exams

Business	Social Sciences
Business Ethics and Society	A History of the Vietnam War
Business Mathematics	Art of the Western World
Computing and Information Technology	Criminal Justice
Human Resource Management	Foundations of Education
Introduction to Business	Fundamentals of Counseling
Management Information Systems	General Anthropology
Money and Banking	History of the Soviet Union
Organizational Behavior	Introduction to Geography
Personal Finance	Introduction to Law Enforcement
Principles of Finance	Lifespan Developmental Psychology
Principles of Supervision	Substance Abuse
	The Civil War and Reconstruction

Humanities	Physical Sciences
Ethics in America	Astronomy
Introduction to World Religions	Environmental Science
Principles of Advanced English	Health and Human Development
Composition	Introduction to Geology
Principles of Public Speaking	

Math	Technology
Fundamentals of College Algebra	Ethics in Technology
Math for Liberal Arts	Fundamentals of Cybersecurity
Principles of Statistics	Technical Writing

As you can see from the table, the DSST program covers a wide variety of subjects. However, it is important to ask two questions before registering for a DSST exam.

1. Which universities or colleges award credit for passing DSST exams?
2. Which DSST exams are the most relevant to my desired degree and my experience?

Knowing which universities offer DSST credit is important. In all likelihood, a college in your area awards credit for DSST exams, but find out before taking an exam by contacting the university directly. Then review the list of DSST exams to determine which ones are most relevant to the degree you are seeking and to your base of knowledge. Schedule an appointment with your college adviser to determine which exams best fit your degree program and which college courses the DSST exams can replace. Advisers should also be able to tell you the minimum score required on the DSST exam to receive university credit.

DSST® TEST CENTERS

You can find DSST testing locations in community colleges and universities across the country. Check the DSST website (**www.getcollegecredit. com**) for a location near you or contact your local college or university to find out if the school administers DSST exams. Keep in mind that some universities and colleges administer DSST exams only to enrolled students. DSST testing is available to men and women in the armed services at more than 500 military installations around the world.

HOW TO REGISTER FOR A DSST® EXAM

Once you have located a nearby DSST testing facility, you need to contact the testing center to find out the exam administration schedule. Many centers are set up to administer tests via the internet, while others use printed materials. Almost all DSST exams are available as online tests, but the method used depends on the testing center. The cost for each DSST exam starts at $85, and many testing locations charge a fee to cover their costs for administering the tests. Credit cards are the only accepted payment method for taking online DSST exams. Credit card, certified check, and money order are acceptable payment methods for paper-and-pencil tests.

Test takers are allotted two score reports—one mailed to them and another mailed to a designated college or university, if requested. Online tests generate unofficial scores at the end of the test session, while individuals taking paper tests must wait four to six weeks for score reports.

PREPARING FOR A DSST® EXAM

Even though you are knowledgeable in a certain subject matter, you should still prepare for the test to ensure you achieve the highest score possible. The first step in studying for a DSST exam is to find out what will be on the specific test you have chosen. Information regarding test content is located on the DSST fact sheets, which can be downloaded at no cost from **www. getcollegecredit.com**. Each fact sheet outlines the topics covered on a subject-matter test, as well as the approximate percentage assigned to each topic. For example, questions on the Technical Writing exam are distributed in the following way: Theory and Practice of Technical Writing–14%, Purpose of Technical Documents–23%, Technical Writing Process–14%, Document Design–18%, and Revising, Editing, and Final Sections–31%.

In addition to the breakdown of topics on a DSST exam, the fact sheet also lists recommended reference materials. If you do not own the recommended books, then check college bookstores. Avoid paying high prices for new textbooks by looking online for used textbooks. Don't panic if you are unable to locate a specific textbook listed on the fact sheet; the textbooks are merely recommendations. Instead, search for comparable books used in university courses on the specific subject. Current editions are ideal, and it is a good idea to use at least two references when studying for a DSST exam. Of course, the subject matter provided in this book will be a sufficient review for most test takers. However, if you need additional information, then it is a good idea to have some of the reference materials at your disposal when preparing for a DSST exam.

Fact sheets include other useful information in addition to a list of reference materials and topics. Each fact sheet includes subject-specific sample questions like those you will encounter on the DSST exam. The sample questions provide an idea of the types of questions you can expect on the exam. Test questions are multiple-choice with one correct answer and three incorrect choices.

The fact sheet also includes information about the number of credit hours ACE has recommended be awarded by colleges for a passing DSST exam score. However, you should keep in mind that not all universities and colleges adhere to the ACE recommendation for DSST credit hours. Some institutions require DSST exam scores higher than the minimum score recommended by ACE. Once you have acquired appropriate reference materials and you have the outline provided on the fact sheet, you are ready to start studying, which is where this book can help.

TEST DAY

After reviewing the material and taking practice tests, you are finally ready to take your DSST exam. Follow these tips for a successful test day experience.

1. **Arrive on time.** Not only is it courteous to arrive on time to the DSST testing facility, but it also allows plenty of time for you to take care of check-in procedures and settle into your surroundings.
2. **Bring identification.** DSST test facilities require that candidates bring a valid government-issued identification card with a current photo and signature. Acceptable forms of identification include a current driver's license, passport, military identification card, or state-issued identification card. Individuals who fail to bring proper identification to the DSST testing facility will not be allowed to take an exam.
3. **Bring the right supplies.** If your exam requires the use of a calculator, you may bring a calculator that meets the specifications. For paper-based exams, you may also bring No. 2 pencils with an eraser and black ballpoint pens. Regardless of the exam methodology, you are NOT allowed to bring reference or study materials, scratch paper, or electronics such as cell phones, personal handheld devices, cameras, alarm wrist watches, or tape recorders to the testing center.
4. **Take the test.** During the exam, take the time to read each question-and-answer option carefully. Eliminate the choices you know are incorrect to narrow the number of potential answers. If a question completely stumps you, take an educated guess and move on—remember that DSSTs are timed; you will have 2 hours to take the exam.

With the proper preparation, DSST exams will save you both time and money. So join the thousands of people who have already reaped the benefits of DSST exams and move closer than ever to your college degree.

TECHNICAL WRITING EXAM FACTS

The DSST® Technical Writing exam consists of 100 multiple-choice questions designed to evaluate whether candidates possess the knowledge and understanding that would be gained by taking a lower-level college course in technical writing, which includes the following content: theory and practice of technical writing; purpose, content, and organizational patterns of common types of technical documents; information design; and technical editing.

Area or Course Equivalent: Technical Writing
Level: Lower-level baccalaureate
Amount of Credit: 3 Semester Hours
Minimum Score: 400
Source: https://www.getcollegecredit.com/wp-content/assets/factsheets/TechnicalWriting.pdf

I. **Theory and Practice of Technical Writing – 14%**

    a. Understanding contexts, purpose(s), and importance

    b. Audience analysis

    c. Ensuring the validity and reliability of data and sources

    d. Establishing the appropriate style

II. **Purpose of Technical Documents – 23%**

    a. Informing

        i. Progress/inspection reports

        ii. Feasibility reports

        iii. Research/laboratory reports

        iv. Instructions, procedures, and process descriptions

    b. Persuading and Making Recommendations

        i. Proposals

        ii. White papers

        iii. Grants

III. **Technical Writing Process – 14%**

    a. Individual and/or collaborative writing

    b. Choice of medium

    c. Drafting and organizing content

    d. Research (primary and secondary)

IV. Document Design – 18%

    a. Elements of document design

        i. Page formatting

        ii. Textual formatting

        iii. Illustration formatting

    b. Strategies of document design

        i. Readability

        ii. Usability

        iii. Accessibility

V. Revising, Editing, and Final Sections – 31%

    a. Revising for

        i. Completeness

        ii. Concision

        iii. Accessibility

        iv. Organization

    b. Editing for

        i. Concision

        ii. Grammatical accuracy

        iii. Technical accuracy

    c. Final sections

        i. Cover letters

        ii. Executive summaries

        iii. Abstracts

Chapter 2

Technical Writing Diagnostic Test

DIAGNOSTIC TEST ANSWER SHEET

1. Ⓐ Ⓑ Ⓒ Ⓓ
2. Ⓐ Ⓑ Ⓒ Ⓓ
3. Ⓐ Ⓑ Ⓒ Ⓓ
4. Ⓐ Ⓑ Ⓒ Ⓓ
5. Ⓐ Ⓑ Ⓒ Ⓓ
6. Ⓐ Ⓑ Ⓒ Ⓓ
7. Ⓐ Ⓑ Ⓒ Ⓓ

8. Ⓐ Ⓑ Ⓒ Ⓓ
9. Ⓐ Ⓑ Ⓒ Ⓓ
10. Ⓐ Ⓑ Ⓒ Ⓓ
11. Ⓐ Ⓑ Ⓒ Ⓓ
12. Ⓐ Ⓑ Ⓒ Ⓓ
13. Ⓐ Ⓑ Ⓒ Ⓓ
14. Ⓐ Ⓑ Ⓒ Ⓓ

15. Ⓐ Ⓑ Ⓒ Ⓓ
16. Ⓐ Ⓑ Ⓒ Ⓓ
17. Ⓐ Ⓑ Ⓒ Ⓓ
18. Ⓐ Ⓑ Ⓒ Ⓓ
19. Ⓐ Ⓑ Ⓒ Ⓓ
20. Ⓐ Ⓑ Ⓒ Ⓓ

TECHNICAL WRITING DIAGNOSTIC TEST
24 minutes—20 questions

Directions: Carefully read each of the following 20 questions. Choose the best answer to each question and fill in the corresponding circle on the answer sheet. The Answer Key and Explanations can be found following this Diagnostic Test.

1. Which of the following summarizes only the scope and purpose of a document?

   A. Informative abstract
   B. Executive summary
   C. Descriptive abstract
   D. Closing summary

2. Which sequencing method would be most appropriate for the description of a new car model?

   A. Spatial
   B. Sequential
   C. Chronological
   D. Cause and effect

3. Which type of proposal would most likely be written by a university professor to request funding from a government agency for a scientific study?

   A. Internal proposal
   B. Sales proposal
   C. Routine proposal
   D. Grant proposal

4. The primary focus of most technical writing is

   A. undocumented opinion.
   B. global integration.
   C. factual information.
   D. supplemental data.

5. Which of the following is written specifically for repair technicians?

    A. User manuals
    B. Training manuals
    C. Service manuals
    D. Operator manuals

6. An informal tone in a document is most appropriate when writing to

    A. colleagues.
    B. customers.
    C. superiors.
    D. academics.

7. It is most appropriate for a technical document conclusion to

    A. interpret findings.
    B. present a new idea.
    C. cite useful references.
    D. define technical terms.

8. Which of the following is true of white papers?

    A. Their purpose is to inform an internal audience about a new project offering.
    B. They do not play a role in a company's branding efforts.
    C. They rely on objective analysis to inform and persuade.
    D. They do not include visual aids.

9. The literal meaning of a word is its

    A. connotation.
    B. subordination.
    C. denotation.
    D. abstraction.

10. All of the following are strategies to promote concise writing EXCEPT:

    A. Eliminating unnecessary words
    B. Repeating major points and key words
    C. Eliminating redundancy
    D. Eliminating superfluous detail

11. A brief definition of a technical term should be explained in a document's

    A. appendix.
    B. glossary.
    C. bibliography.
    D. table of contents.

12. Which of the following would most likely be written when a business is considering the development of a new service?

    A. Feasibility report
    B. Internal memo
    C. Progress report
    D. Solicited proposal

13. Which of the following involves the use of a synonym to explain the meaning of an unfamiliar word?

    A. Sentence definition
    B. Expanded definition
    C. Parenthetical definition
    D. Definition by components

14. The major difference between instructions and procedures is that procedures are intended for

    A. unskilled users.
    B. groups of people.
    C. sales personnel.
    D. new employees.

15. Learning as much as possible about the readers of a technical document is known as audience

    A. purpose.
    B. analysis.
    C. planning.
    D. adaptation.

16. Below, some part of the sentence or the entire sentence is underlined. Beneath this sentence, you will find four ways of phrasing the underlined part. Choice A repeats the original; the other three are different. If you think the original is better than any of the alternatives, choose choice A. Otherwise, choose one of the others. In choosing answers, pay attention to grammatical correctness, appropriate word choice, and smoothness and effectiveness of sentence construction.

Prior to welding, <u>a visual inspection at 1X magnification will be performed and the surface is smooth and clean.</u>

    A. Prior to welding, a visual inspection at 1X magnification will be performed and the surface is smooth and clean.

    B. Prior to welding, a visual inspection at 1X magnification will be performed to ensure the surface is smooth and clean.

    C. Prior to welding, a visual inspection at 1X magnification will be performed so the surface is smooth and clean.

    D. Prior to welding, a visual inspection at 1X magnification will be performed, yet the surface is smooth and clean.

17. Which of the following graphics is best for tracing steps in a process?

    A. Table
    B. Flowchart
    C. Pie chart
    D. Line graph

18. All of the following are elements of most laboratory reports EXCEPT:

    A. Costs
    B. Results
    C. Equipment
    D. Procedures

19. Which of the following demonstrates proper parallel structure?

    A. The goal of this progress report is to update management about current system upgrades, problems that have pushed back the timeline for the upgrade, and to present a revised timeline for project completion.

    B. The goal of this progress report is to update management about current system upgrades and problems that have pushed back the timeline for the upgrade. It also presents a revised timeline for project completion.

    C. Both A and B

    D. Neither A nor B

20. All of the following are true of executive summaries EXCEPT:

    A. Their length will vary, depending on the length of the document they summarize

    B. They highlight important points from all major document sections

    C. They are often persuasive

    D. They are part of a document's back matter

ANSWER KEY AND EXPLANATIONS

1. C	**5.** C	**9.** C	**13.** C	**17.** B
2. A	**6.** A	**10.** B	**14.** B	**18.** A
3. D	**7.** A	**11.** B	**15.** B	**19.** B
4. C	**8.** C	**12.** A	**16.** B	**20.** D

1. **The correct answer is C.** A descriptive abstract summarizes in a few sentences the scope and purpose of a document. An informative abstract (choice A) summarizes an entire report, not only the scope and purpose. Executive and closing summaries (choices B and D) review the main points of a document.

2. **The correct answer is A.** The spatial method of development is used to describe the physical appearance of something, such as a new car. The sequential method (choice B) is for explaining systematic instructions. Chronological order (choice C) explains a sequence of events, such as a car accident. The description of a car involves no cause-and-effect relationship, so choice D is incorrect.

3. **The correct answer is D.** A professor requesting funding from the government for a study would submit a grant proposal. Internal and routine proposals (choices A and C) are submitted within organizations. A sales proposal (choice B) is used to gain business.

4. **The correct answer is C.** Presenting facts is the main focus of technical documents. Technical documents may include expert opinions and supplemental data, such as statistics, but essential facts are the focal point. Technical writers need to consider whether a document will be read on a global level, but global integration is not a key consideration.

5. **The correct answer is C.** Service manuals contain troubleshooting charts to help diagnose equipment problems. These manuals are specifically written for repair technicians. User manuals (choice A) are written for the people who use a product, not repair it. Training manuals (choice B) are used as teaching tools with certain vocations, and operator manuals (choice D) are for trained equipment operators.

6. **The correct answer is A.** An informal tone in technical writing is appropriate for colleagues and subordinates in most cases. Superiors and academics, such as professors, require a formal or semiformal tone. A semiformal or formal tone is also appropriate when communicating with customers.

7. **The correct answer is A.** The conclusion of a technical document should interpret findings presented in the report. New ideas (choice B) should not be introduced in a conclusion. References (choice C) are cited in a bibliography. Technical terms (choice D) are typically defined in the body of a document.

8. **The correct answer is C.** White papers rely on objective analysis, research, and a thorough, informative treatment of paper content. Choice A is incorrect because the audience for a white paper is external, not internal. The opposite of choice B is true. White papers are often used for marketing purposes or to sell information or products. The opposite of choice D is true as well. White papers will often include visual aids to help make the technical content accessible to laypersons.

9. **The correct answer is C.** The denotation of a word is its literal meaning or dictionary definition. A word's connotation (choice A) is the associations it brings to mind for different people, which may be positive or negative. *Subordination* (choice B) and *abstraction* (choice D) have no relation to the literal meaning of words.

10. **The correct answer is B.** Concise writing eliminates unnecessary words and details. These elements are considered unnecessary if they do not clarify the main point of a document. Choices A, C, and D are all strategies designed to trim sentence content that does not clarify a main point. Choice B, on the other hand, offers a strategy to promote unity within a document.

11. **The correct answer is B.** The glossary is where technical and unfamiliar terms are defined. An appendix (choice A) includes additional information and can include expanded definitions where appropriate. However, the glossary is where you would find a brief definition of a term. A bibliography (choice C) cites references used for a document. A table of contents (choice D) lists where information is located in a report or proposal.

12. **The correct answer is A.** Feasibility reports are written when a business is considering a major change, such as developing a new service or moving a manufacturing facility. Memos (choice B) are written to request information or announce policies within an organization. Progress reports (choice C) describe the status of a large project. Solicited proposals (choice D) are persuasive documents written to earn business.

13. **The correct answer is C.** Parenthetical definition involves using a synonym or phrase to explain the meaning of an unfamiliar term in a document. Sentence definitions (choice A) and expanded definitions (choice B) are lengthier than a word or phrase. A definition by components (choice D) is a type of expanded definition.

14. **The correct answer is B.** Procedures are used to clarify the rules and expectations that group members should follow in different situations. Instructions are the steps taken to complete a task. The opposite of choice A is correct. Choices C and D are not the primary focus of procedures.

15. **The correct answer is B.** Audience analysis refers to gathering information about the readers of a technical document in preparation for writing. The purpose of a technical document is an important aspect of writing preparation, but the terms *purpose* (choice A) and *planning* (choice C) do not describe audience analysis. Choice D is incorrect because technical writers often adapt their messages *after* learning about the needs and knowledge of readers.

16. **The correct answer is B.** The original sentence exhibits faulty coordination, meaning that both coordinate clauses are positioned as equal when in reality they contain unequal ideas. Choice B converts "the surface is smooth and clean" into a subordinate clause. Although choice C likewise converts the second clause into a subordinate one, the use of *so* incorrectly implies that the clean surface is the result of the inspection. The use of *yet* in choice D inappropriately introduces a change in the direction of the logic.

17. **The correct answer is B.** Flowcharts are appropriate for tracing the steps or decisions in any type of procedure or process. A table (choice A) helps organize explanations and numbers. Pie charts (choice C) relate parts to the whole. Line graphs (choice D) show changes over time.

18. **The correct answer is A.** Results, equipment, and procedures are key elements usually included in laboratory reports. In order for a test to be repeatable, an author must identify all equipment and procedures used. The costs associated with laboratory testing are not included in a laboratory report in most instances.

19. **The correct answer is B.** The third item in the list presented in choice A exhibits a different grammatical structure from the first two list items. Choice B corrects the problem by splitting the long sentence into two.

20. **The correct answer is D.** An executive summary precedes a technical document so it is part of its front matter. Unlike an abstract which remains consistent in length, regardless of the length of the document it summarizes, an executive summary should be approximately 10 percent of the length of the original document, so a longer document requires a longer executive summary. Its structure mirrors the document's structure and each section of an executive summary presents summary content from each section. Their purpose is often persuasive as an executive summary is often the only portion of a document that a decision maker will read.

DIAGNOSTIC TEST ASSESSMENT GRID

Now that you've completed the diagnostic test and read through the answer explanations, you can use your results to target your studying. Find the question numbers from the diagnostic test that you answered incorrectly and highlight or circle them below. Then focus extra attention on the sections dealing with those topics.

Technical Writing

Content Area	Topic	Question #
Theory and Practice of Technical Writing	• Understanding contexts, purpose, and importance • Audience analysis • Ensuring the validity and reliability of data and sources • Establishing the appropriate style	4, 6, 15
Purpose of Technical Documents	• Informing • Persuading and making recommendations	3, 5, 8, 14, 18
Technical Writing Process	• Individual and/or collaborative writing • Choice of medium • Drafting and organizing content • Research (primary and secondary)	2, 7, 9
Document Design	• Elements of document design • Strategies of document design	11, 12, 13, 17
Revising, Editing, and Final Sections	• Revising • Editing • Final sections	1, 10, 16, 19, 20

Chapter 3

Technical Writing Subject Review

OVERVIEW

- Theory and Practice of Technical Writing
- The Purpose of Technical Documents
- The Technical Writing Process
- Document Design
- Revising, Editing, and Final Sections
- Summing It Up

THEORY AND PRACTICE OF TECHNICAL WRITING

Technical writing refers to any written communication pertaining to a job, such as manuals, instructions, reports, and proposals. Although the subject is usually technical, any document that contains industry-specific language is a type of technical writing. Almost every career involves an element of technical writing—science, engineering, business, health sciences, and technology. Doctors maintain patient records, scientists write lab reports, software engineers write manuals, and managers write personnel evaluations. Understanding the specific elements of technical communication is essential in the information-driven twenty-first century. On your DSST Technical Writing exam, about 14 percent of the questions you see will cover the theory and practice of technical writing.

Understanding Context, Purpose, and Importance

Technical documents are generally targeted for a specific audience—a technician who is hired to repair malfunctioning computer equipment might be the audience for a procedural manual. A busy executive who must make a decision to invest in new computers might be the audience for a technical proposal.

Just as different technical documents are written for different audiences, they are also written for different purposes. A process description might help the technician understand the steps involved in repairing broken computers while a formal proposal might convince the CEO to purchase new computers instead of repairing the broken ones.

To make sure that they reach their intended audience and achieve their purpose, technical documents are well-organized and highly-structured. Often, they contain visual aids to reinforce their message. The writing style is concise and the tone is objective. This means that unlike essays written for class or poetry written for pleasure, technical writing focuses on facts rather than personal thoughts, feelings, and attitudes.

Purpose

Purpose refers to what a technical writer wants the reader to know, believe, or do after reading a piece of technical writing. The two most common purposes for technical documents are as follows:

Technical Purpose		
Purpose	**Definition**	**Example Document Types**
Inform	Teaches a reader about a particular topic	• Manuals • Process or mechanism descriptions • Instruction sheets • Fact sheets • Progress reports • Research/lab reports • Incident reports • Feasibility reports
Persuade	Convinces a reader to take action or adopt a specific perspective	• Proposals • White papers • Grants

As the table implies, an **informative document** helps readers learn information. **Persuasive documents** make recommendations and encourage readers to take action or adopt a specific point of view. Many types of technical documents may achieve either (or both) purposes, depending on the situation.

To determine the purpose of a technical document, writers should ask the following questions:

- What action do I want people to take after reading the document?
- What do I want to convince readers of?
- What do I want people to know after reading the document?
- Do I want my readers to learn something, buy something, or change their minds about something?

The answers to these questions should be as specific as possible to simplify the writing task and to guarantee that the document achieves the writer's goal.

Audience and Audience Analysis

The **audience** refers to the intended reader (or readers) of a technical document. In order for technical writing to achieve its purpose the author must consider the audience's point of view. In fact, the audience should be the chief consideration when planning and writing a technical document.

To make sure they are properly considering their audience, technical writers conduct an audience analysis. **Audience analysis** refers to learning as much as possible about the individuals who will use a specific document. Understanding the knowledge, interests, and needs of readers enables a writer to adapt a message and tailor it to the specific audience.

One important factor is the technical experience of the reader. Readers with different levels of technical experience require different amounts of explanation and technical detail. The technical background of the audience determines whether terms need to be explained. As shown in the following table, readers who have a technical background and who are familiar with the subject of a technical document need only straightforward data, but those unfamiliar with terminology expect interpretations and recommendations.

Audience Technicality Level

Document User	Necessary Information	Example
Highly technical	Audience consists of experts in the subject matter; data does not require lengthy explanation	A physician giving a report to a surgeon about a patient's lab results and symptoms
Semi-technical	Audience consists of people with some technical knowledge but less than experts; data needs some explanation	A physician giving a report to first-year medical students regarding a patient's lab results and symptoms
Nontechnical	Audience consists of laypersons with no training in the subject matter; data needs to be translated into simple language that can be easily understood	A physician giving a report to a patient's spouse regarding lab results, symptoms, and treatment options

The following are additional important items to consider when conducting an audience analysis:

Audience Analysis

Question	Based on the Answer:
Is the reader a technical expert, proficient in technical material, or a layperson?	• Determine appropriate level of technical detail and amount of explanation needed • Determine whether it is appropriate to use technical language (jargon) • Determine whether to use visual aids
How much does the reader know about the topic?	• Provide a brief summary of content that is well-known to readers • Add detail or explanation about topics that readers are unfamiliar with
How interested is the reader in the topic?	• Use knowledge of interests to determine what content to include in technical document

Audience Analysis

Question	Based on the Answer:
Does the reader share the author's point of view or priorities?	• Determine what evidence would convince the reader to agree • Determine what information would appeal to the reader's priorities or perspective
What role does the reader play and what will he or she need to do after reading the document?	• Write different content for people who play different roles—for example, provide technical details for technicians; include information on the bottom line and associated risks and benefits for decision makers • Determine what tone is appropriate for the audience—adopt a formal tone with executives or supervisors; use a semiformal or informal tone with peers or subordinates
What is the reader's background/culture/belief system	• Consider whether and how these factors are likely to impact your reader's perception of your writing style or content
What is the reader's personality or learning preference?	• Determine appropriate tone • Determine appropriate medium (formal or informal proposal) • Include many facts and present them in a logical order for analytical readers • Focus on the big picture for creative readers
Will the audience consist of more than one type of reader?	• Consider whether to include supplemental sections, such as glossaries or appendixes

Evaluating Data Validity and Reliability

Technical writers often conduct research so they can include data or evidence in their documents. **Evidence** refers to any information used to support or refute a claim. Ethical technical writers strive for balanced evidence, which means they avoid exaggeration and include all pertinent information. Factual statements, statistics, and expert opinions are examples of hard, verifiable evidence. **Soft evidence** refers to uninformed opinions and unverified data.

Before writing any technical document, a technical writer must evaluate the information and evidence that will be included to ensure it is valid and reliable. Thus, he or she must carefully choose which sources of information to include. A printed source or electronic content published by a university or other respected organization is most likely reliable. A source found on the internet may or may not be.

To determine whether a source is reliable, consider the following guidelines:

Evaluating Sources of Evidence		
Area of Focus	Questions	Concerns
Author	• Who wrote the source? • What is the author's perspective? • What are the author's credentials and expertise?	• Is the author an expert in the field? • Is the source objective? • Is the information reliable?
Document Purpose	• What does the author want a reader to do after reviewing the content? • Why was the content created? • What is the website's sponsor and domain type (i.e., .edu, .com, .gov, .net)?	• Is the information biased? • Is the information being used to facilitate profit or information sharing?
Publication	• Who published the source? • Is the document peer-reviewed? • Was the content self-published?	• Is the information reliable? • Is the information accurate?
Format	• What medium does the author use?	• Is the format appropriate for the audience?
Relevance	• Is the information related to the document? • Do facts and figures support the document's point of view?	• Is the content appropriate for the audience? • Is the evidence presented likely to convince an audience? • Is the author presenting himself as a credible researcher?

Evaluating Sources of Evidence

Area of Focus	Questions	Concerns
Publication Date	• When was the source written? • Has information been updated?	• Is the information current? The source of the information should be as current as possible, although some information changes very quickly. Information regarding technology is often outdated in a few months, so a document about diabetes treatments or data mining requires the most current research. (NOTE: Some topics, such as workplace ethics and flexible scheduling, benefit from including both recent and historical research.)
Credibility	• Does the author cite sources? • What sources did the author cite? • What kind of links does the author include on the web page?	• Is the author ethical? • Is the information reliable? • Is the information biased?

For the most valid data, technical writers should avoid relying on a single source to provide information and should instead acquire a consensus from many different sources.

Establishing the Appropriate Style

Although different types of writing may address the same or similar subjects, the approach differs depending on the type of writing. A personal essay, for example, is expressive writing that shares the author's experience, observations, or feelings. A research paper, on the other hand, does not convey information gathered from personal experience; rather, it discusses information discovered through study. A personal essay on the topic of animal rights might focus on the fact that the author felt upset and angry after witnessing animal abuse. Meanwhile, an informative, research-based essay on the same subject might discuss what animal rights activists have published on the subject of the ethical treatment of animals.

Technical writing often shares information that a reader needs to understand a specific topic or perform an action. It might require library or field research (information gathered from surveys or questionnaires) or scientific study. Regardless of the purpose, technical writing requires a writer to present information precisely, accurately, and objectively.

Tone

The attitude expressed by a writer toward a subject is the **tone** of a document. For technical writing, tone depends on the purpose, audience, and method of communication. Tone indicates the distance between a writer and a reader; it also indicates the attitude of the author toward the topic and the audience. Although no rules exist for determining the most appropriate tone for a technical document, the following guidelines may be useful to writers:

- Use a formal or semiformal tone when the writing is intended for superiors or professionals.
- Use a semiformal or informal tone when the writing is intended for colleagues and subordinates.
- Use an informal tone when a conversational style is desired, but avoid being too informal with profanity, slang, or poor grammar.

THE PURPOSE OF TECHNICAL DOCUMENTS

The purpose of a technical document refers to the goal that the author wants to accomplish. Different types of technical documents have different purposes. This section discusses some of the most common document types and their purposes—on your exam, around 23 percent of the questions you face will ask you about the purpose of technical documents.

Documents That Inform

Reports

Reports often provide the basis for decision making in the workplace, and they may be formal, informal, informational, or analytical:

- **Informational reports** focus on providing straightforward information—results of a customer survey, minutes of a department meeting, or profits and losses for the month.

- **Analytical reports** evaluate information, draw conclusions, and make recommendations.
- **Formal reports** are typically lengthy, require extensive research, and involve multiple writers.
- **Informal reports** lack extensive planning or research, and they often take the form of a memorandum.

Executives and employees write numerous types of reports in the workplace, but progress reports, feasibility reports, and laboratory reports are the focus of this review.

Progress reports, also known as **status reports**, keep the reader informed about activities, problems, and progress related to a large project. A project involving numerous steps may require the submission of regular progress reports—daily, weekly, or monthly. Progress reports are extremely useful in managerial decisions regarding work schedules, task assignments, funding, and supplies.

When writing a progress report, it is important for technical writers to think about the reader's questions and consider which ones are most important. The following table lists some of questions that clients and managers often expect progress reports to answer. It also contains advice for how to organize a progress report and cultivate an informative tone.

Progress Report Overview		
Questions	Organization	Tone/Content
Which tasks have been completed?	• Use lists, headings, and subheadings when discussing multiple tasks	• Use past tense • Be detailed, clear, and accurate
Which tasks must be completed in the future?	• Use lists, headings, and subheadings when discussing multiple tasks	• Use future tense
What problems have impacted the work?	• Use lists or describe any problems in paragraph format	• Describe items impacting work quality • Describe project obstacles • Be honest • Report facts, avoid placing blame
When will all tasks be complete?	• Consider using a chart or table to outline the timeline	• If problems have stalled progress, provide a new anticipated completion date

The structure of a progress report often depends on the business, and many companies have specific forms they require for progress reports. However, every progress report pertaining to the same project should be organized in the same manner for the sake of consistency. In general, the first progress report submitted for a project includes an introduction or overview that states the project, necessary materials, and anticipated completion date. Follow-up reports explain what work has been completed, what work remains to be done, scheduling information, budget updates, and recommendations.

When a business considers the purchase of new equipment, development of a new product, or relocation of manufacturing facilities, executives initially attempt to assess the likelihood that the project or change will succeed. **Feasibility reports** help executives determine if an idea or a plan is both possible and practical. In some cases, a course of action may be possible but impractical because it would lower productivity or raise costs. Feasibility reports should address a variety of questions:

- Is this plan likely to succeed?
- What are the benefits and risks of the plan?
- What are other options?
- Is funding available?
- How would employees be affected?

Feasibility reports often begin with a purpose statement, such as, "The purpose of this report is to determine the feasibility of moving our manufacturing facilities overseas." The length of a feasibility report depends on the size of the project, but most follow a similar structure:

- **Introduction:** contains background information and purpose statement
- **Body:** presents a review of options being considered based on carefully selected evaluation criteria such as costs and resources needed
- **Conclusion:** presents an interpretation of the findings
- **Recommendation:** provides the author's opinion regarding the most feasible option based on the criteria discussed in the body of the report

Although the structure and length of feasibility reports varies, they should always review possible alternatives, provide specific recommendations, and include enough details to support the author's recommendations.

Laboratory reports relay information gathered from an investigation or from laboratory testing. The format of a laboratory report varies by profession and organization, but basic elements exist in almost all laboratory reports:

- The reason for conducting the test or investigation
- Equipment and procedures used during the investigation
- Problems, results, and conclusions

The most critical aspect of laboratory reports is the equipment and procedures used during testing. Duplicating the test and assessing the accuracy of the investigation depend upon the equipment used and the procedures followed.

Manuals

Manuals are documents that help people understand how to assemble, use, and repair products. Nearly every product sold to consumers—from waffle irons to automobiles—includes a manual. Different types of manuals serve a variety of purposes and audiences.

Types of Manuals

Type	Purpose and Audience
User Manuals	Written for both skilled and unskilled users of a product; include instructions regarding setup, operation, and maintenance as well as safety warnings and troubleshooting tips
Tutorials	Written as a self-study guide for the users of a product; intended to guide first-time users through the steps involved in operating a product
Training Manuals	Major teaching tool in vocational jobs; used to train people in a procedure or skill and often paired with audiovisual information
Operators Manuals	Written for trained operators of construction, computer, or manufacturing equipment for use on the job; includes instructions and safety information
Service Manuals	Written for repair technicians; contain troubleshooting charts for diagnosing problems

Before writing a manual, an author must consider whether the typical reader is a novice user, intermediate user, or expert user of the product or service. Audience determines the details to include and the terminology to use.

Instructions and Procedures

Instructions and procedures are two aspects of technical documentation that require clarification because they are frequently confused. **Instructions** are the steps required to complete a specific task safely and efficiently, such as installing a memory card into a laptop. People who have never performed a certain task are the typical audience for instructions. Printed manuals, online documentation, and brief reference cards are examples of common instructional documents. Instructional documents must be written accurately because consumers who are injured by a product due to faulty instructions may sue the technical writer. The misuse of power tools, medications, and cleaning products can lead to serious injuries, so all safety information and potential risks must be clearly explained to users in instructional documents.

Instructions that act as guidelines for people familiar with a task are called **procedures**. Procedures ensure safety within a group. For example, most businesses have written safety procedures that explain how to evacuate a building during a fire. Safety procedures include how to assist personnel with special needs, where to meet after evacuation, and who to contact for assistance. Written procedures also help maintain consistency. For example, police departments have specific procedures to follow when investigating a crime scene to ensure that officers gather, label, and store evidence correctly. Procedures help members of a group learn the expectations and rules related to a specific task.

Process Descriptions

A **process description** or a **process explanation** describes how something works and breaks down a process into steps or parts. The steps required to manufacture a DVD or the way a bank reviews loan applications are both typical subjects of process explanations. Well-written process descriptions include enough details so another person is able to follow the process through each step.

A process description begins with an introduction that provides an overview of the process or explains the importance of learning the process. Defining terminology and including visual aids helps make the process clear for readers. A technical writer clarifies each step of a process with transitional phrases and topic headings that indicate to readers that one stage is complete, and another is beginning.

A conclusion wraps up the process description by summarizing the major stages and describing a complete cycle of the process.

An item or process is best described in a specific order to enable the audience to understand. Technical writers use spatial sequence to describe a mechanism at rest and to explain what an object is, what it does, and what it looks like. Technical writers use functional sequence when describing a mechanism that is in action and discussing how a mechanism works. When describing the order of assembly and explaining how a mechanism is put together, technical writers use chronological sequence. (For more information on sequence patterns, see the *Revising, Editing, and Final Sections* subject review at the end of this chapter.)

Documents That Persuade/Make Recommendations

Proposals

Proposals are documents written to persuade readers to take some type of action. The intention of a proposal may be to offer a solution to an identified need or organizational problem, persuade an audience to support a plan, authorize a project, or purchase a product. Reports and proposals have similar elements, but they differ in purpose. Although the recommendations section of a report may be somewhat persuasive, the majority of a report is informative. In contrast, a proposal is entirely persuasive in nature.

While numerous types of proposals are used in the workplace, the organizational pattern, formality, and length of each kind varies. An internal proposal is submitted to personnel within an organization; an external or sales proposal is submitted to clients or potential customers. Short proposals include an introduction, body, and conclusion. In contrast, long proposals are divided into front matter, body, and back matter. **Front matter** refers to the content that precedes the main proposal and includes the cover letter, title page, table of contents, and list of figures. The **body** includes the executive summary, introduction, problem description, rationale, cost analysis, personnel expertise, statement of responsibilities, organizational sales pitch, request for approval, and the conclusion. **Back matter** refers to the content that follows the main proposal content; it includes appendixes, a bibliography, and a glossary of terms.

Types of Proposals

Type	Purpose and Audience
Routine internal proposal	Written in short proposal format; used frequently in organizations for minor spending requests
Formal internal proposal	Internal proposal used when requesting large amounts of money
Solicited proposal	External proposal written in response to a request for proposals (RFP) or an invitation for bids (IFB)
Unsolicited proposal	External proposal written and submitted without request
Sales proposal	External proposal that may be short or long depending on size of potential sale
Grant or research proposal	External proposal written to request funding for a project or study

White Papers

A **white paper** is a document that an organization uses to present its position on an issue to an audience outside the organization or to propose a solution for a pressing problem to potential clients. They are considered persuasive because they are often used for marketing purposes or to sell information or products. Often, potential clients consider white papers when making decisions about which solution represents their best option.

White papers can be difficult to write because they are written for diverse, often unknown audiences. For example, they may be written for the general public or for companies that might be searching for a solution to a particular problem. Even though writers of white papers may not know their audience well, they must focus on reader needs if they hope to convince people that their proposed solution or perspective is valid.

Even though white papers play a role in the sales and marketing process, they rely on objective analysis, research, and a thorough, informative treatment of paper content. Writers of white papers must be mindful to balance informative and persuasive content and avoid producing a document that reads like a technical report or sales brochure.

While the structure of a white paper may vary depending on the organization and context, there are certain techniques that you as a writer may use to achieve both an objective tone and a persuasive purpose:

- Focus on benefits.
- Use informative illustrations and other visuals to emphasize written content.
- Discuss topics from the reader's perspective.
- Focus on problem solving or the ways in which a particular product might address a need.
- Include evidence from subject matter experts and scientific or research studies.
- Use headings to help readers follow the discussion.
- Consider alternative solutions or perspectives.
- Document research properly.

Grant Proposals

Grant proposals are written to request funding for a specific project or study. Often, they require technical writers to address very specific content and follow explicit instructions so that **grantmakers** (organizations that provide funds to grant winners) can expedite the proposal review process. Reviewers are not likely to read past the point where proposals demonstrate a lack of compliance with instructions, so attention to detail is critical.

Although the structure and content of grant proposals vary depending on the grantmaker's instructions, grant writers can expect to provide a cover letter and an executive summary and include the following content:

- Problem statement
- Work schedule
- Budget
- Qualifications
- Conclusions
- Appendices

Further, grant writers must strive to be as clear and specific as possible while adhering to limits set by grantmakers.

THE TECHNICAL WRITING PROCESS

Like all writing, technical writing is a process. This means that there are steps that technical writers must take to express and refine their ideas. On the DSST Technical Writing exam, around 14 percent of exam questions will ask you about the technical writing process.

Generally, the steps of the technical writing process are as follows:

- **Planning**—analyzing audience; determining structure, purpose, scope, and content
- **Researching**—gathering the information to be discussed in a technical document
- **Drafting**—producing a technical document that will later be refined after team or individual review
- **Revising**—determining whether additions or changes are needed to the content or structure of a technical document
- **Editing**—determining whether a technical document is grammatically and technically correct
- **Publishing**—delivering the technical content to the audience

The process is by no means linear; writers often perform many of these steps out of order or repeat steps as needed. For example, a writer who is in the drafting phase may discover that more research is needed to inform or persuade an audience.

Individual and Collaborative Writing

Technical documents may be written by individuals or project teams. When technical documents are often long and complex, they are frequently written by project teams as opposed to individual authors. When more than one person authors a technical document they are engaged in **collaborative writing**. Collaborative writing requires technical authors to navigate the challenges presented by the complex writing process and the challenges of collaboration. It therefore requires strong communication and interpersonal skills.

Collaborative writing requires that project teams complete a number of tasks to help them stay organized and avoid obstacles. They include:

- Establishing an agenda and common goal
- Identifying writing tasks and dividing those tasks among members of the project team

- Identifying roles for group members
- Tracking ideas
- Developing a system for document management and version control
- Managing conflict

Planning and preparing a technical document can be challenging in a collaborative environment. Team members should consult with one another and meet regularly to discuss ideas and ensure that the document reflects the entire team's decisions.

Further, different writers have different styles, so creating a consistent voice and strong links between independently developed pieces of content can be difficult. A collaborative document requires heavy editing to standardize the writing style and tone, and weave the content together in a visually and linguistically cohesive document. Generally, this work is completed by a single person, referred to as an editor or a revision manager.

Choice of Medium

Medium refers to the way in which technical writers communicate information in a technical document. More specifically, it refers to the way in which the writing will be delivered. For example, an informal report that is composed using the memo form might be delivered by email. Writers should consider the context and the audience's expectations when choosing a medium. Official correspondences and formal communications should be included as attachments to emails or distributed in paper format while informal communications might be included in the body of an email message.

Drafting and Organizing Technical Content

Technical documents are often lengthy, so it is common for writers to include a summary of information, introduction, conclusion, definitions, and report supplements to aid readers.

Introductions

The purpose of an **introduction** is to help the reader understand the scope, purpose, and structure of a technical document. An effective introduction captures the reader's attention and provides enough context to help the reader understand what he or she will read in the body and supporting sections of the document.

Conclusions

The purpose of a **conclusion** in a technical document is to summarize information, interpret findings, and offer recommendations. Conclusions offer an author a final opportunity to emphasize a significant point that will remain with the reader. Throughout a document, writers explain evidence, but the conclusion sums up the analysis and leads to a recommendation—if the document requires the author's opinion.

Depending on the type of document, a conclusion should have certain characteristics:

- **Summary:** represents the main points of the document
- **Interpretation:** coincides with findings presented in the document
- **Recommendations:** agree with purpose, evidence, and interpretations of the document

The purpose of the document and the reader's needs dictate the content of a conclusion. For example, a report may end with a recommendation, yet it may be more advantageous to conclude a sales proposal with a persuasive statement regarding the benefits of purchasing a product. Other methods of effectively concluding a document involve ending with a thought-provoking statement or quotation, asking readers to take action, making predictions, and presenting ideas to consider. Regardless of the approach used to conclude a document, writers should never introduce a new topic. Conclusions should always refer to the information and ideas presented in the document.

Definitions

Defining unfamiliar terms and concepts is critical for the clarity of a technical document. **Definitions** help readers understand the precise meaning of a word, concept, or process. Within various types of technical documents, definitions may have legal implications. For example, contracts and employee handbooks require clear definitions to ensure that all parties understand the legal terms and responsibilities. Technical writers employ a variety of methods when defining terms in documents.

Methods for Defining Terms

Definition Type	Description
Parenthetical definition	Uses a synonym or a clarifying phrase to explain the meaning of an unfamiliar word; easy to set up links in electronic documents
Sentence definition	Used for complex terms or when a term has multiple meanings; follows a fixed pattern: indicate the item to be defined, the class in which the item belongs, and the features that make the item unique from others in same class
Expanded definition	Used when extensive details are required about an item; may be a paragraph or numerous pages depending on the audience and purpose

Parenthetical and sentence definitions are appropriate when a reader only requires a general understanding of a term or a concept. However, expanded definitions may be necessary when a reader needs to know how something works or when a reader is semi-technical or nontechnical. Definitions can be expanded in a variety of ways:

- **Etymology:** describe the term's origin, such as Greek or Latin words
- **Background:** discuss history, development, and applications for the term, unless readers are only attempting to perform a task related to the term
- **Negation:** explain what the term does not mean
- **Operation:** explain how an item or process works
- **Analysis of parts:** explain how each element of a complex item works, which is especially beneficial to laypersons attempting to understand a technical subject
- **Visuals:** show the meaning of a process or concept
- **Comparison and contrast:** compare or contrast unfamiliar information with information the reader understands
- **Examples:** use those that match a reader's level of comprehension to describe how an item is used or how it works

Including definitions in a document promotes reader understanding but determining where to place definitions can be tricky. If four or fewer terms need to be explained, then parenthetical definitions or hypertext links are appropriate because the flow of the text will not be disrupted.

However, more than four terms requiring clarification calls for sentence definitions placed in the glossary of the document. Expanded definitions belong in the introduction if the term is essential to understanding the entire document. An expanded definition that explains a major point belongs in that specific section. An appendix is appropriate for an expanded definition that is merely a reference in a document and not essential to understanding a key point.

Report Supplements

Long documents need to be accessible to readers who may not have the time or interest to read the full text. As such, report supplements are beneficial tools. Like formal proposals, long documents have both front matter and back matter. The table of contents is part of the front matter, and the glossary and appendixes are part of the back matter.

Table of Contents

A formal document longer than ten pages usually includes a table of contents to simplify the process of locating information. Most writers place the table of contents after the title page and abstract but before the list of tables, the foreword, and the preface. A **table of contents** shows what is contained in a document and on what pages information can be located. In the table of contents, list the major headings of a document in the order in which they appear and include subheadings as well. Front matter is listed in Roman numerals, and page numbers begin with the first page of the report, most likely the introduction.

Glossary

The **glossary** of a document is an alphabetical listing of definitions. Technical terms, or those that have a unique meaning in the document, require definitions for reader comprehension. A glossary defines technical terms without breaking the flow of a document. Technical documents intended for laypersons may require a glossary, yet an audience of skilled readers may not need technical terms defined at all. In general, a document containing more than five technical terms calls for a glossary. Explain the meaning of five or fewer technical terms either within the text or in a footnote. Definitions should be concise and clear to enhance reader understanding. Insert a glossary after the appendixes and the bibliography in the back matter of a long document.

Appendix

An **appendix** is part of the back matter of a document, and it serves the purpose of clarifying or supplementing information presented in the text's body. Documents may contain more than one appendix, but each appendix should address only one piece of information. Arrange multiple appendixes in a document in the order in which the information appears in the body. Each appendix begins on a new page and is identified with a letter (beginning with A) and an appropriate title. A document containing only one appendix does not require letters, only *Appendix* as the title. The following is a list of typical information that would be appropriate for an appendix:

- Experiment details
- Complicated formulas
- Interview questions and answers
- Quotations longer than one page
- Maps and photographs
- Sample questionnaires, tests, and surveys
- Large visual aids

Keep in mind that information is generally included in an appendix if it would interfere with the main body text or is too detailed or lengthy for the primary reader. However, writers should not include irrelevant information in appendixes or use too many of them.

Research

Technical writers often conduct research so that they have enough valid data to support their conclusions and recommendations. There are two types of research that may assist technical writers in gathering appropriate data.

Primary Research

Primary research refers to any data that writers collect themselves. Examples of primary research include surveys, questionnaires, interviews, or recorded observations about people, events, or products. The following questions can help guide technical writers in conducting primary research:

- What do I want or expect to find out?
- How will I go about finding out what I want to know? What methods will I use? (This is referred to as a **research methodology**.)

- What do I know or believe about this topic? (The goal is to identify biases and think about ways to keep them from influencing your research methods.)
- Who am I going to speak with or study? (The people you will observe or question are referred to as research subjects or participants.)
- How will I find people to participate in my study?

Once information is gathered, technical writers analyze and organize the information based on criteria that they develop so that they can look for patterns or gain a deeper understanding of how a product or process works.

Secondary Research

Secondary research refers to a review of the studies that other people conducted and the data they gathered and analyzed as a result of those studies. It is useful when technical writers need to understand what is already known about a topic or what possible solutions exist to solve a complicated problem. Secondary research is sometimes used to help prepare a technical writer for primary research. Conducting secondary research can help a technical writer identify what data is needed or what research methods would be the most effective. Often, it is the only kind of research that a technical writer will perform.

DOCUMENT DESIGN

It's often said that appearance is everything, and for technical documents—whether a report, memo, manual, proposal, or email—this is definitely true. The proper use of titles and headings, page design, and visuals is extremely important when writing and composing technical documents. Document design questions will comprise about 18 percent of your DSST Technical Writing exam.

Elements of, and Strategies for, Design

Page design can emphasize certain aspects of a document and visually indicate the organization of information. Authors should keep readers in mind when designing pages and focus on using page design elements consistently throughout a document. The following elements of page design are effective tools for enhancing the appearance of a technical document.

Page Design Elements

Design Element	Description
Justification	Margins justified on the left are easier to read; fully justified appropriate for multiple columns.
Headings	Indicate organizational structure and help readers find information; type size or font should differ from main text.
Lists	Useful in presenting steps, materials, and recommendations.
Headers and footers	Often include section topic, date, page number, and title of document.
Columns	Single-column for larger typeface; double for smaller typeface. Avoid orphans and widows. **Orphan** is a word on a line by itself at the end of a column. **Widow** is a single line carried over to the top of a column.
Color	Useful in highlighting sections of a document to draw reader attention.
White space	Blank space between paragraphs and between sections visually helps readers know when one idea or section is beginning or ending.

Readers often base their decision to read a technical document upon the **title**. Well-written titles indicate a variety of information about a document—topic (the subject of the technical document), tone, scope (what topics are included and what level of detail is provided in a technical document), purpose, and more. The most useful titles are concise yet specific. Avoid sentence form and redundancies in titles. The subject line acts as the title for memos and emails.

Within the body of a technical document, **headings** serve as titles of sections and subtopics. Headings have a number of purposes, especially in lengthy reports:

- Help readers find a particular section
- Divide information into logical pieces
- Highlight main points and topics
- Signal topic changes

Headings can be real time-savers for readers and make a technical document more accessible. The way in which a heading is phrased depends on its function in the document. A **topic heading** is a brief phrase or word that is most appropriate when there are many subtopics in a document; however, they can be too vague for readers. **Statement headings** require a sentence or a detailed phrase and are useful when a specific detail about a topic needs to be addressed. **Question headings** draw readers into the topic, but they may be too informal for some documents.

Visuals also improve a document's readability and appearance. A technical writer who needs to explain an idea more clearly than is possible with words will often turn to visuals. Drawings, photographs, and maps show readers what something looks like. Graphs and tables illustrate numbers and quantities. Flowcharts, diagrams, and organizational charts clarify relationships.

As with most elements of technical writing, audience and purpose determine what visuals should be utilized in a document. For example, numerical tables and schematics are most appropriate for expert readers who are able to interpret information sufficiently. Basic graphs and diagrams are suitable for audiences with limited technical knowledge.

In general, technical writers use visuals when readers need to focus on a particular idea. Visuals serve to instruct or persuade the reader, and they draw the reader's attention to an important concept. Including visuals is also beneficial when an author anticipates that a document will be consulted by readers unfamiliar with the topic or by readers who only need to read specific sections of a document.

Types of Visuals	
Type	**Description**
Tables	Data organized for easy comparison
Bar graphs	Translate numbers into shapes or colors; show comparisons
Line graphs	Show trends and changes over time, cost, size, rates, and other variables
Pie charts	Show parts of a whole
Gantt charts	Show how the phases of a project relate to each other
Pictograms	Use images or icons to represent quantities; useful for nonexperts to grasp ideas

Types of Visuals	
Type	**Description**
Flowcharts	Show steps in a process
Schematic diagrams	Show how components of a principle, process, or system function together
Drawings	Show real or imaginary objects; highlight specific parts; use exploded view to show how parts fit together

Visuals are especially effective when placed near the text they are clarifying. Especially large or lengthy visuals should be included in an appendix.

REVISING, EDITING, AND FINAL SECTIONS

If the appearance and content of a technical document are sound, but the writing is not readable, then the writer has not met the audience's needs. Thus, revising and editing are important steps in writing technical documents. **Revision** considers whether a document is complete, properly scoped, appropriate for the audience, and well-structured. **Editing** considers whether a document is grammatically correct, properly formatted, and free of typos, broken hyperlinks, spelling mistakes, and sentence-level errors. Some tasks, such as considering whether a document is concisely written, occur during both levels of review. Questions that cover revising, editing, and final sections will make up about 31 percent of your DSST Technical Writing exam.

Completeness

When technical writers consider whether their documents are **complete**, they evaluate whether they have treated their topic thoroughly enough. Specifically, they consider whether they have provided all necessary information to the reader, whether they have addressed all the questions they posed in the planning stages or anticipated questions a reader might have, and whether additional content is needed to ensure a document meets its purpose. Some questions writers can use to assess completeness are as follows:

- Has the document's purpose been fulfilled? Why or why not?
- Does the body of the document provide all the information required to understand the conclusion, recommendation, or results? If not, does the document provide guidance as to where readers can find the necessary information (e.g., is the information located in an appendix)?

- Does the document provide enough evidence to support important findings, recommendations, or results?
- What questions will the audience have after reading the document?

Conciseness

Writing with **conciseness** involves removing unnecessary words, phrases, and sentences from a document without impeding clarity. Concise does not necessarily mean brief, because lengthy reports may be concise. Two kinds of wordiness plague documents. One type of wordiness involves giving readers unnecessary information. Another kind involves using too many words to convey relevant information. Use the fewest words possible to express a concept, but do not omit information that is required for clarity.

Wordiness is a normal occurrence during draft writing, but editing should repair the problem. For example, eliminate phrases like "basic and fundamental" or "each and every" because they bog down a document with redundancies. Excess qualification, such as "completely accurate," adds to the wordiness of a document as well. Introductory phrases like "in order to," "due to the fact that," and "through the use of" can be easily replaced with single words—*to*, *because*, and *by*. Another way to achieve conciseness is by using parallel sentence structure. Such a structure requires elements of a sentence to be similar in function and grammatical form. Parallelism enhances meaning, achieves emphasis, and eliminates wordiness as indicated in the following examples:

- **Not parallel:** Our new SUV has other features such as a moon roof, a DVD player, and switching to four-wheel drive.
- **Parallel:** Our new SUV has other features such as a moon roof, a DVD player, and a four-wheel drive option.

Parallel sentence structure is especially important when developing outlines, and creating tables of contents because it helps readers understand how the different parts of a document are related.

Accessibility and Organization

Accessibility refers to how easy it is for a writer to read a technical document, follow its logic, and comprehend its content. An accessible document is one that is well organized and clear. Effective formatting and heading use can also contribute to document accessibility.

Unity and Sequence

The **unity** of a document refers to its single purpose and its presentation of information. A paragraph that exhibits unity pertains to one idea and does not deviate from it. When editing a technical document, an author needs to question whether each paragraph concentrates on a single topic, whether the entire document focuses on achieving one purpose, and whether all ideas flow logically together.

Information presented in a logical sequence creates a readable document. Certain **sequence patterns**, or **methods of development**, are useful when creating technical documents.

Sequence Patterns	
Method	**Description**
Spatial	Describes the physical appearance of an object or area beginning at one point and ending at another; useful for product or mechanism descriptions
Chronological	Follows sequence of events; useful for explanations of how something is done or how an accident occurred
Sequential	Used for writing step-by-step instructions
Cause and Effect	Begins with either the cause or the effect; useful in reports discussing problems and solutions
Emphatic	Emphasizes important information; reasons or examples are arranged in decreasing or increasing order of importance; used when making recommendations or proposals
Comparison	Used when writing about one subject that is similar to another

Most writers blend various methods of development or use more than one in a single document. During the editing process, writers need to consider the unity of each paragraph and the way in which the paragraphs and sections link together.

Transitional Phrases

Transitional phrases are like road signs that help the reader understand the logic of a technical document. They build unity and clarify the connection between different sections of a document. The smooth flow of ideas within a paragraph or between paragraphs is accomplished with the use of appropriate transitions. Readers are more easily able to make connections and understand the relationships between concepts when an author uses transitions in a document. Creating unity with transitions can be achieved in a number of ways:

- Using transitional words and phrases
- Repeating major points or key words
- Summarizing information presented in a previous paragraph
- Using numbers to indicate steps in a process (first, second, third)

The following table presents some common transition words and phrases.

Transitional Words and Phrases

Transition Type	Purpose	Examples
Additions	Provide evidence and further explanation	Moreover; furthermore; besides; again; and; in addition; equally importantly; another example
Contrast	Shows a change in the direction of the logic	But; yet; however; still; nevertheless; on the other hand; on the contrary; in contrast; at the same time; although
Comparison	Shows similarities between points or examples	Similarly; likewise; in the same way
Clarification	Explain a point	In other words; to restate; put another way; indeed; in short; for example; for instance; to illustrate; such as
Results	Signals discussion of findings	Thus; as a result; therefore; hence; consequently; subsequently
Time	Indicates a time relationship, sequence, or chronology	Meanwhile; immediately; shortly; afterward; later; after a few minutes (hours, weeks, months, years, etc.); first (second, third, etc.); finally
Summary	Conclude, summarize, restate ideas	In summary; on the whole; in short; as stated; in conclusion

Clarity

A logical presentation of information and clearly written sentences improve the overall **clarity** of a technical document. Editing for clarity requires focusing on sentence construction and word choice. Avoid ambiguity with clear phrasing, appropriate punctuation, and agreement between pronouns and antecedents.

Proper word choice also promotes clarity because choosing a precise word helps technical writers avoid vagueness. To be precise, technical writers must be aware of the denotation and connotation of words. The **denotation** of a word is its literal meaning, or the definition found in a dictionary. The **connotation** of a word refers to the associations that a word has—both positive and negative. For example, the denotative meaning of *school* is a building where people receive an education, but the connotative meaning varies. For some people, school may generate negative memories of difficult classes, but other people may think about fun experiences with friends. Words used in technical documents should have precise denotations and appropriate connotations for both the audience and purpose.

Emphasis and subordination are likewise necessary for clarity in writing. Stressing important ideas by positioning key words or ideas first or last in a sentence is known as **emphasis**. By organizing information in a paragraph from familiar to unfamiliar, a writer is also able to place emphasis on a key concept. **Subordination** in a sentence shows that a less important concept is dependent upon a more important concept. Subordinating conjunctions, such as *because, if, while, which,* and *since* indicate relationships in a sentence:

- A sedentary lifestyle is linked to obesity. A lack of exercise also puts people at risk for high blood pressure. (The two ideas are equally important.)
- A sedentary lifestyle, which is a risk factor for high blood pressure, is linked to obesity. (The risk factor for high blood pressure is subordinated, and the link to obesity is emphasized.)
- A sedentary lifestyle, which is linked to obesity, is a risk factor for high blood pressure. (The risk factor for obesity is subordinated, and the link to high blood pressure is emphasized.)

Failure to use emphasis and subordination will result in clauses and sentences that have equal importance in a document. Readers will be required to determine which concepts are most important, and their assumptions may not be what the author intended.

Accuracy

If an organization presents flawed or erroneous information in a technical document, its credibility suffers and the organization may be subjected to unwanted consequences. As mentioned earlier, readers might sue if they suffer injury as a result of reviewing inaccurate information; it is important that a subject matter expert reviews a document for technical accuracy. Some areas of focus are as follows:

- Facts are correct and derived from credible sources.
- Evidence supports the claims made.
- Third-party review occurs when information is in dispute.
- Limitations are noted—for example, the reviewer of a proposal for IT support considers whether a proposed solution only pertains to specific hardware or software.
- Written procedures are tested for completeness, ease of use, and accuracy.

During the editing process, a technical writer or editor also reviews a document for errors such as wrong words, missing words, misspelled words, punctuation issues, subject-verb agreement, and other problems related to writing mechanics. Grammatical review occurs as follows:

- **Personal review:** technical writers review their own work
- **Peer review:** a colleague or technical editor is called upon to review the work
- **Technological review:** spelling and grammar checking programs are used to review work

Grammatical review is important as readers often make judgments about an author's attention to detail or writing ability when they encounter writing-related errors.

Final Sections

Cover Letters

Just like job seekers use cover letters to introduce themselves and their qualifications to potential employers, technical writers use cover letters to introduce the audience to a document and its ideas or recommendations. The cover letter is often the first piece of writing that a decision maker or potential client sees, so it is important to make a strong first impression. This is particularly true of proposals.

The purpose of a proposal is to facilitate a sale or propose a solution to a problem. A **cover letter** assists in the fulfilment of that purpose by enticing the reader to review the executive summary and enough of the body of the proposal that they are convinced the ideas it proposes represent the best possible solutions for his or her organization.

A technical writer cannot be sure if an audience will read further than the cover letter so it is important that the cover letter provide a concise, clear summary of a document's content. As the cover letter should be no longer than a page, a technical writer should prioritize and include only the one or two most important points. To assist in identifying those points, a technical writer might ask the following question:

- What would I tell the readers if I only had one minute to educate them about my solution, findings, or recommendation?

For a proposal cover letter, the answer to this question should focus heavily on the following:

- Solutions for the potential client's problem or needs
- The benefits that the solution would offer to the potential client

A cover letter is a formal document and so it should be presented on business letterhead, properly formatted with a header, a date of submission, and a greeting. If the technical writer does not know the recipient of the document well, a formal greeting (such as "Dear Mr./Ms.") should be used. The reader's first name can be used if the writer knows the recipient well and regularly uses that form of address.

The content of a cover letter varies depending on the organization and context. However, it generally contains the following content:

- Overview of the problem
- Overview of the proposed solution, recommendation, or findings
- Contact information

For documents with a persuasive purpose, the cover letter should also provide insight into proposal benefits and a call to action—or a statement of what the writer hopes the reader will do after reviewing the document.

Summaries and Abstracts

Closing summaries, executive summaries, informative abstracts, and descriptive abstracts are four types of summarized information often included in technical documents. The following table provides description and placement information.

Summaries and Abstracts

Type	Description
Closing summary	Included either at the beginning of the conclusion or at the end of the body; reviews main points and findings
Executive summary	Included before full report; combines main points of a report or proposal; often persuasive
Informative abstract	Included before full report; summarized version of report
Descriptive abstract	Included on the title page; summarizes in a few sentences the scope and purpose of the document

Informative abstracts and executive summaries are often confused because they are similar. An **abstract** is a summary of a written document that enables readers to determine whether to read an entire article. An **executive summary** combines the main points of a report or proposal, and it is often the only section of a longer document that is read. Executive summaries follow the same sequence as the full document with subheadings to assist the reader. Most executive summaries are 10 percent of the length of the original document, while most abstracts are approximately 200 words long, regardless of the length of the original article.

SUMMING IT UP

- **Technical writing** is any written communication pertaining to a job—manuals, instructions, reports, and proposals. Most technical communication helps readers understand a process, concept, or technology.
- **Audience analysis** means learning about the individuals who will use a specific document—their technical and cultural backgrounds, experience and training, attitudes about subject matter, and needs and interests.
- The **sources** and **evidence** used in a technical document should be both valid and reliable. For the most valid data, avoid relying on a single source for information and instead acquire a consensus from many different sources. A printed source published by a university or other respected organization is most likely reliable.
- **Progress** or **status reports** keep readers informed about activities, problems, and steps forward related to a large project, whether on a daily, weekly, or monthly basis.
- **Feasibility reports** help executives determine if an idea or a plan is possible and practical. They should review possible alternatives, provide specific recommendations, and include details to support the author's recommendations.
- **Laboratory reports** relay information gathered from an investigation or laboratory testing, including the reason for conducting the investigation, equipment and procedures used, and problems, results, and conclusions.
- **Manuals** (user, tutorial, training, operator, and service) help people understand how to assemble, use, and repair products. An author must consider whether the reader is a novice, intermediate, or expert user of the product or service.
- **Instructions** are the steps required to complete a specific task safely and efficiently. People who have never performed a certain task are the typical audience for instructions, which must be accurately written to avoid causing injuries to consumers.
- **Procedures** are instructions that act as guidelines for people familiar with a task. Safety procedures include how to assist personnel with special needs, where to meet after evacuation, and who to contact for assistance.
- A **process description** or **explanation** describes how something works. **Spatial sequence** is used to describe a mechanism at rest. **Functional sequence** is used to describe a mechanism in action. **Chronological sequence** is used to describe the order of assembly.

- **Proposals** persuade readers to take some type of action. Long proposals are divided into front matter (cover letter, title page, table of contents, and list of figures), body (executive summary, introduction, problem description, rationale, cost analysis, personnel expertise, statement of responsibilities, organizational sales pitch, request for approval, and conclusion), and back matter (appendixes, bibliography, and glossary of terms).
- A **white paper** is a document that an organization uses to present its position on an issue to an audience outside the organization or to propose a solution for a pressing problem to potential clients. They are considered persuasive because they are often used for marketing purposes or to sell information or products.
- **Grant proposals** are written to request funding for a specific project or study. Often, they require technical writers to address very specific content and follow explicit instructions so that grantmakers (organizations that provide funds to grant winners) can expedite the proposal review process.
- **Technical documents** may be written by individuals or project teams. When technical documents are often long and complex, they are frequently written by project teams as opposed to individual authors. When more than one person authors a technical document they are engaged in collaborative writing. **Collaborative writing** requires technical authors to navigate the challenges presented by the complex writing process and the challenges of collaboration. It requires strong communication and interpersonal skills.
- **Medium** refers to the way in which technical writers communicate information in a technical document. More specifically, it refers to the way in which the writing will be delivered.
- Technical writers often conduct **research** so that they have enough valid data to support their conclusions and recommendations. There are two types of research that may assist technical writers in gathering appropriate data— **primary** and **secondary research**.
- The purpose of a **conclusion** in a technical document is to summarize information, interpret findings, and offer recommendations.
- **Definitions** help readers understand the meaning of a word, concept, or process. Use parenthetical definitions for four or fewer terms. Place expanded definitions in the introduction if the term is essential to understanding the entire document or in an appendix if not essential to understanding a key point. Use sentence definitions if more than four terms require clarification and place them in the glossary.
- **Headings** serve as titles of sections and subtopics within the body of a technical document.

- **Page design elements** include justification, headings, lists, headers, footers, columns, color, and white space.
- **Audience** and **purpose** determine which visuals should be used in a document. Numerical tables and schematics are best for expert readers; basic graphs and diagrams are best for those with limited technical knowledge.
- For technical writing, **tone** (a writer's attitude toward a subject) depends on the purpose, audience, and method of communication. Use a formal or semiformal tone for superiors or professionals, a semiformal or informal tone for colleagues and subordinates, and an informal tone when a conversational style is desired.
- **Information sequence methods** include spatial, chronological, sequential, cause and effect, emphatic, and comparison.
- A word's **denotation** is its literal meaning; **connotation** refers to the word's positive and negative associations.
- When technical writers consider whether their documents are **complete**, they evaluate whether they have treated their topic thoroughly enough. Specifically, they consider whether they have provided all necessary information to the reader, whether they have addressed all the questions they posed in the planning stages or anticipated questions a reader might have, and whether additional content is needed to ensure a document meets its purpose.
- **Concise** writing involves removing unnecessary words, phrases, and sentences without impeding clarity. Check for parallel sentence structure so that elements of a sentence are similar in function and grammatical form.
- **Accessibility** refers to how easy it is for a reader to read a technical document, follow its logic, and comprehend its content. An accessible document is one that is well organized and clear. Unity, sequencing, transitions, and clarity all contribute to a document's accessibility.
- The **unity** of a document refers to its single purpose and its presentation of information. A paragraph that exhibits unity adheres to one idea and does not deviate from it.
- **Transitional phrases** are like road signs that help the reader understand the logic of a technical document. They build unity and clarify the connection between different sections of a document.
- If an organization presents **flawed or erroneous** information in a technical document, its credibility suffers, and the organization may be subjected to unwanted consequences. It is important that documents be reviewed for technical accuracy by a subject matter expert.

- **Grammatical review** is important as readers often make judgments about an author's attention to detail or writing ability when they encounter writing-related errors.
- Technical writers use a **cover letter** to introduce the audience to a document and its ideas or recommendations. The cover letter is often the first piece of writing that a decision maker or potential client sees, so it is important to make a strong first impression.
- **Closing summaries, executive summaries, informative abstracts**, and **descriptive abstracts** are four types of summarized information often included in technical documents. An executive summary combines the main points of a report or proposal and is often the only section of a longer document that is read.

Chapter 4

Technical Writing Post-Test

POST-TEST ANSWER SHEET

1. Ⓐ Ⓑ Ⓒ Ⓓ
2. Ⓐ Ⓑ Ⓒ Ⓓ
3. Ⓐ Ⓑ Ⓒ Ⓓ
4. Ⓐ Ⓑ Ⓒ Ⓓ
5. Ⓐ Ⓑ Ⓒ Ⓓ
6. Ⓐ Ⓑ Ⓒ Ⓓ
7. Ⓐ Ⓑ Ⓒ Ⓓ
8. Ⓐ Ⓑ Ⓒ Ⓓ
9. Ⓐ Ⓑ Ⓒ Ⓓ
10. Ⓐ Ⓑ Ⓒ Ⓓ
11. Ⓐ Ⓑ Ⓒ Ⓓ
12. Ⓐ Ⓑ Ⓒ Ⓓ
13. Ⓐ Ⓑ Ⓒ Ⓓ
14. Ⓐ Ⓑ Ⓒ Ⓓ
15. Ⓐ Ⓑ Ⓒ Ⓓ

16. Ⓐ Ⓑ Ⓒ Ⓓ
17. Ⓐ Ⓑ Ⓒ Ⓓ
18. Ⓐ Ⓑ Ⓒ Ⓓ
19. Ⓐ Ⓑ Ⓒ Ⓓ
20. Ⓐ Ⓑ Ⓒ Ⓓ
21. Ⓐ Ⓑ Ⓒ Ⓓ
22. Ⓐ Ⓑ Ⓒ Ⓓ
23. Ⓐ Ⓑ Ⓒ Ⓓ
24. Ⓐ Ⓑ Ⓒ Ⓓ
25. Ⓐ Ⓑ Ⓒ Ⓓ
26. Ⓐ Ⓑ Ⓒ Ⓓ
27. Ⓐ Ⓑ Ⓒ Ⓓ
28. Ⓐ Ⓑ Ⓒ Ⓓ
29. Ⓐ Ⓑ Ⓒ Ⓓ
30. Ⓐ Ⓑ Ⓒ Ⓓ

31. Ⓐ Ⓑ Ⓒ Ⓓ
32. Ⓐ Ⓑ Ⓒ Ⓓ
33. Ⓐ Ⓑ Ⓒ Ⓓ
34. Ⓐ Ⓑ Ⓒ Ⓓ
35. Ⓐ Ⓑ Ⓒ Ⓓ
36. Ⓐ Ⓑ Ⓒ Ⓓ
37. Ⓐ Ⓑ Ⓒ Ⓓ
38. Ⓐ Ⓑ Ⓒ Ⓓ
39. Ⓐ Ⓑ Ⓒ Ⓓ
40. Ⓐ Ⓑ Ⓒ Ⓓ
41. Ⓐ Ⓑ Ⓒ Ⓓ
42. Ⓐ Ⓑ Ⓒ Ⓓ
43. Ⓐ Ⓑ Ⓒ Ⓓ
44. Ⓐ Ⓑ Ⓒ Ⓓ
45. Ⓐ Ⓑ Ⓒ Ⓓ

46. Ⓐ Ⓑ Ⓒ Ⓓ   **51.** Ⓐ Ⓑ Ⓒ Ⓓ   **56.** Ⓐ Ⓑ Ⓒ Ⓓ

47. Ⓐ Ⓑ Ⓒ Ⓓ   **52.** Ⓐ Ⓑ Ⓒ Ⓓ   **57.** Ⓐ Ⓑ Ⓒ Ⓓ

48. Ⓐ Ⓑ Ⓒ Ⓓ   **53.** Ⓐ Ⓑ Ⓒ Ⓓ   **58.** Ⓐ Ⓑ Ⓒ Ⓓ

49. Ⓐ Ⓑ Ⓒ Ⓓ   **54.** Ⓐ Ⓑ Ⓒ Ⓓ   **59.** Ⓐ Ⓑ Ⓒ Ⓓ

50. Ⓐ Ⓑ Ⓒ Ⓓ   **55.** Ⓐ Ⓑ Ⓒ Ⓓ   **60.** Ⓐ Ⓑ Ⓒ Ⓓ

TECHNICAL WRITING POST-TEST
72 minutes—60 questions

Directions: Carefully read each of the following 60 questions. Choose the best answer to each question and fill in the corresponding circle on the answer sheet. The Answer Key and Explanations can be found following this post-test.

---

1. Which of the following transitions is most appropriate for indicating a logical relationship between two ideas?

    A. Meanwhile
    B. Therefore
    C. Furthermore
    D. Specifically

2. The type of report that provides information regarding which tasks of a large project need to be completed is a(n)

    A. investigative report.
    B. feasibility report.
    C. progress report.
    D. test report.

3. All of the following are examples of white space EXCEPT:

    A. Margins
    B. Space between paragraphs
    C. Headers
    D. Gutters

4. All of the following are true of secondary research EXCEPT:

    A. It focuses solely on firsthand data, such as personal interviews or recorded observations.
    B. It can help researchers conduct more thorough primary research.
    C. It requires the use of reliable and credible sources.
    D. It is sometimes the only kind of research a technical writer performs.

5. All of the following are questions that a technical writer could use to evaluate a laboratory report for completeness EXCEPT:

   A. Are the recommendations justified?
   B. Is the purpose of the report clear?
   C. Is there enough evidence to support the findings in the analysis section?
   D. Will the audience have questions about the research methods section?

6. Which of the following may be too informal for a proposal?

   A. Question headings
   B. Statement headings
   C. Minor topic headings
   D. Major topic headings

7. Modifying the language used in a document to make it suitable for specific readers is an example of

   A. abstracted information.
   B. audience adaptation.
   C. documented research.
   D. audience analysis.

8. The primary purpose of a progress report is to

   A. report on a change in a project timeline.
   B. recommend a change in procedure.
   C. report on project completion.
   D. persuade a supervisor to approve additional resources for a project.

9. Which of the following does NOT need revision to correct an error in parallel structure?

A. Although the exact cause of diabetes is uncertain, medical experts believe that both heredity and environment are significant factors.

B. Achilles tendinitis is common among individuals who either play sports, such as basketball, or that suddenly increase the frequency of exercise.

C. People diagnosed with epilepsy usually take medication to reduce the frequency, intensity, and a dangerous accident related to a seizure.

D. Food and airborne allergies can cause symptoms that affect the skin, sinuses, digestive system, and breathing ability.

10. Which of the following does NOT require revision to correct an error in parallel structure?

A. Mass defect—or loss—occurs when protons and neutrons combine to form a nucleus.

B. The software was neither Windows compatible nor was it UNIX compatible.

C. The Hepatitis B virus is transmitted through blood, causes inflammation of the liver, and associated symptoms are flu-like in nature.

D. The Antikythera mechanism was used to predict eclipses, track the lunar calendar, and many people consider it the first analog computer.

11. Feasibility reports are most often written to help determine whether an idea is

A. successful and profitable.

B. necessary and reliable.

C. possible and practical.

D. new and promising.

In items 12 and 13, some part of the sentence or the entire sentence is underlined. Beneath each sentence, you will find four ways of phrasing the underlined part. Choice A repeats the original; the other three are different. If you think the original is better than any of the alternatives, choose answer A. Otherwise, choose one of the others. In selecting answers, pay attention to grammatical correctness, appropriate word choice, and smoothness and effectiveness of sentence construction.

12. <u>Symptoms of lupus include a low red blood cell count and swollen feet and hands.</u>

   A. Symptoms of lupus include a low red blood cell count and swollen feet and hands.
   B. People who suffer from lupus often have a low red blood cell count and show signs of swelling in the feet and hands.
   C. Symptoms of lupus include anemia and edema.
   D. Symptoms of lupus include a low red blood cell count as well as swollen feet and hands.

13. <u>Following the experiment</u>, the laboratory assistant reported that the sample showed no signs of contamination.

   A. Following the experiment, the laboratory assistant reported that the sample showed no signs of contamination.
   B. The laboratory assistant following the experiment reported that the sample showed no signs of contamination.
   C. The laboratory assistant reported following the experiment that the sample showed no signs of contamination.
   D. The laboratory assistant reported that the sample showed no signs of contamination following the experiment.

14. Equipment and procedures must be included in a laboratory report for the purpose of

   A. understanding results.
   B. duplicating the test.
   C. explaining the data.
   D. recalling information.

15. Which of the following should be addressed when editing an informal sales proposal for computer software solutions?

A. The proposal does not note that its solution is not compatible with LINUX operating systems.

B. The following sentence appears in the executive summary: "With a virtual desktop application, Company X can improve it's mobile computing capabilities by 59 percent."

C. Both A and B

D. Neither A nor B

In items 16–18, some part of the sentence or the entire sentence is underlined. Beneath each sentence, you will find four ways of phrasing the underlined part. Choice A repeats the original; the other three are different. If you think the original is better than any of the alternatives, choose answer A. Otherwise, choose one of the others. In selecting answers, pay attention to grammatical correctness, appropriate word choice, and smoothness and effectiveness of sentence construction.

---

16. Natural gas is often found in coal beds where it was created by microorganisms, and it consists mostly of methane.

A. Natural gas is often found in coal beds where it was created by microorganisms, and it consists mostly of methane.

B. Natural gas, which consists mostly of methane, is often found in coal beds where it was created by microorganisms.

C. Natural gas is often found in coal beds, was created by microorganisms, and consists mostly of methane.

D. Natural gas is often found in coal beds and consists mostly of methane where it was created by microorganisms.

17. The new arena next to the highway is touted for its state-of-the-art design.

A. The new arena next to the highway is touted for its state of-the-art design.

B. The new arena is next to the highway, and it is touted for its state-of-the-art design.

C. The new arena is touted for a state-of-the-art design, and it is located next to the highway.

D. The new arena, touted for its state-of-the-art design, is next to the highway.

18. The vice president was wrongly accused <u>of mishandling the firm's largest marketing project by the stockholders.</u>

    A. of mishandling the firm's largest marketing project by the stockholders.
    B. by the firm's largest marketing project of mishandling the stockholders.
    C. of mishandling by the stockholders in the firm's largest marketing project.
    D. by the stockholders of mishandling the firm's largest marketing project.

19. The main difference between laboratory reports and feasibility reports is that feasibility reports include

    A. informal language.
    B. instructions.
    C. test results.
    D. recommendations.

20. A document intended for an audience of subject matter experts would most likely be written in language that is

    A. highly technical.
    B. semi-technical.
    C. indefinite.
    D. subjective.

21. Clarity in a technical document can best be achieved by

    A. using abstract terms.
    B. eliminating transitions.
    C. including many appendixes.
    D. writing in parallel structure.

22. A word on a line by itself at the end of a column is known as a(n)

    A. orphan.
    B. header.
    C. outlier.
    D. widow.

23. A memo regarding salary cuts would most likely be organized

    A. functionally.
    B. indirectly.
    C. spatially.
    D. directly.

24. Which of the following visuals would be appropriate to use when showing steps in a process?

    I. Flowchart
    II. Schematic diagram
    III. Representational diagram

    A. I only
    B. III only
    C. I and II only
    D. I, II, and III

25. The glossary of a technical document is typically placed

    A. in an appendix.
    B. before the introduction.
    C. in the front matter.
    D. after the bibliography.

26. A visual that shows how the phases of a project relate to one another is known as a

    A. prose table.
    B. pictogram.
    C. bar graph.
    D. Gantt chart.

27. What is the purpose of the conclusion in a feasibility report?

    A. Express an opinion
    B. Interpret the findings
    C. Introduce alternatives
    D. Review the costs

28. All of the following are methods for improving the unity of a document EXCEPT:

A. Using transitions.
B. Repeating key points.
C. Using enumeration.
D. Explaining word origins.

29. A technical writer who wants to show what percentage of total monthly sales was generated by each department would most likely use a(n)

A. tree chart.
B. pie graph.
C. line graph.
D. organizational chart.

30. Which of the following visuals is most appropriate for nontechnical readers?

A. Multiline graph
B. Schematic diagram
C. Pictogram
D. PERT chart

31. All of the following are elements of the audience to consider when writing technical documents EXCEPT:

A. Methods
B. Attitude
C. Needs
D. Culture

32. What is the customary place in a document to include a descriptive abstract?

A. At the end of the body
B. In the conclusion
C. On the title page
D. In the appendix

33. Which of the following is included in the back matter of a long proposal?

A. Bibliography
B. Cost analysis
C. Conclusion
D. Rationale

34. A line graph is most appropriate for showing

A. parts of a whole.
B. changes over time.
C. phases of a project.
D. sequence of events.

35. Unlike other types of technical documents, proposals are primarily written to

A. persuade readers.
B. describe products.
C. analyze audiences.
D. compare options.

36. Which of the following guidelines applies to preparing appendixes for a technical document?

A. Use numbers to identify appendixes.
B. Use a separate appendix for each major item.
C. Limit each appendix to one page in length.
D. Arrange appendixes in order of importance.

37. The conclusion of a sales proposal would most likely include

A. a discussion of a competitor's weaknesses.
B. persuasive statistics not presented in the body.
C. background information about procedures used.
D. a persuasive statement about a company's strengths.

38. Which of the following is written to request approval for hiring an additional part-time employee?

A. Formal internal proposal
B. Progress report
C. Routine internal proposal
D. Feasibility report

Questions 39 and 40 refer to the following group of numbered sentences:

1. Every spot holds many identical DNA strands.
2. The spots reflect a unique DNA sequence and represents one gene.
3. A microarray is a technique that scientists use to evaluate whether genes are turned on and off
4. Computer databases are used to keep track of the DNA sequence and position of each spot.
5. Rows and columns comprising thousands of spots are arranged on a glass surface.

39. If the sentences are reorganized into a cohesive paragraph, which represents the fourth sentence?

A. 1
B. 3
C. 4
D. 2

40. Which transition word or phrase should be used to join sentences 1 and 2?

A. However
B. And
C. In sum
D. For example

41. Information in a technical document is best divided into logical pieces by

A. titles.
B. headings.
C. footers.
D. headers.

42. A status report provides information about accomplishments related to

A. multiple departments in an organization.
B. multiple projects in a given period.
C. one employee in an organization.
D. one project during a given period.

43. Which section of a long proposal is most often the only one read by an audience?

A. Costs
B. Methods
C. Executive Summary
D. Statement of Problem

44. Which of the following is the best way to determine the reliability of a printed source?

A. Publisher
B. Readability
C. Soft evidence
D. Publication date

45. Which of the following is the primary benefit of headings in a technical document?

A. Improve readability
B. Clarify style and tone
C. Enhance visual design
D. Summarize main points

46. Feasibility reports should include all of the following EXCEPT:

A. A review of all alternatives
B. Specific recommendations
C. Procedures and instructions
D. An interpretation of various options

47. Which of the following is content appropriate for a grant proposal?

A. Problem statement
B. Budget and schedule
C. Qualifications
D. All of the above

48. In which of the following situations would a drawing be most appropriate to include in a report?

A. To record the development of an event over time
B. To save space and add visual appeal for laypersons
C. To show cutaway views of internal mechanisms
D. To show distances and locations of specific sites

49. A cover letter for a formal proposal composed in response to an RFP should contain all of the following EXCEPT:

   A. Concise overview of the solution
   B. Formal salutation and professional closing
   C. Summary of benefits for the client
   D. Paragraph describing the features of the solution

50. Which of the following sentences does NOT need to be revised for clarity?

   A. The CEO told human resources many times that the firm needed another sales agent.
   B. Being so familiar with medical equipment, I would appreciate your assistance with the sales presentation for the pediatric clinic.
   C. The office manager resents the vice president because he performed poorly during the first quarter of the year.
   D. All active-duty police officers are not required to submit daily trip reports.

51. Terms included in a document's glossary are

   A. limited to technological concepts.
   B. listed in the order they appear.
   C. arranged alphabetically.
   D. explained in full detail.

52. Which of the following would a trained bulldozer driver use to review safety procedures?

   A. Tutorials
   B. Service manual
   C. Training manual
   D. Operator manual

53. Which of the following communication situations would require writers to establish a common goal, manage conflict, and develop a system for version control?

A. A progress report written by a project manager to update management on a change to the project schedule

B. A sales proposal written by a team of subject matter experts in response to a government request for proposal (RFP)

C. A description of a new performance review process written by the HR manager

D. An informal sales proposal written by a sales associate for a well-known client

54. Which of the following elements of a long proposal would include the problem statement?

A. Product description

B. Cost analysis

C. Background

D. Site preparation

55. Which of the following best indicates what an author wants a reader to know, believe, or do after reading a technical document?

A. Executive summary

B. Topic

C. Purpose statement

D. Outline

56. The main difference between an informative abstract and an executive summary is that executive summaries are

A. presented orally.

B. slightly persuasive.

C. placed in the conclusion.

D. always 200–250 words.

57. Which of the following most improves the validity of information used in a technical document?

A. Statistical data

B. Website graphics

C. Multiple sources

D. Website sponsorship

58. The front matter of a long proposal includes all of the following EXCEPT:

A. Title page
B. Introduction
C. Cover letter
D. List of figures

59. The major difference between procedures and manuals is that manuals

A. assert opinions.
B. specify actions.
C. discuss results.
D. provide guidelines.

60. When writing an informative abstract, assume that the audience consists of

A. readers with different levels of knowledge.
B. academics from different subject areas.
C. highly technical subject-matter experts.
D. readers with no technical interests.

ANSWER KEY AND EXPLANATIONS

1. B	**13.** D	**25.** D	**37.** D	**49.** D
2. C	**14.** B	**26.** D	**38.** C	**50.** A
3. C	**15.** C	**27.** B	**39.** D	**51.** C
4. A	**16.** B	**28.** D	**40.** B	**52.** D
5. B	**17.** D	**29.** B	**41.** B	**53.** B
6. A	**18.** D	**30.** C	**42.** D	**54.** C
7. B	**19.** D	**31.** A	**43.** C	**55.** C
8. C	**20.** A	**32.** C	**44.** A	**56.** B
9. A	**21.** D	**33.** A	**45.** A	**57.** C
10. A	**22.** A	**34.** B	**46.** C	**58.** B
11. C	**23.** B	**35.** A	**47.** D	**59.** D
12. A	**24.** C	**36.** B	**48.** C	**60.** A

1. **The correct answer is B.** Transitions such as *therefore, consequently,* and *as a result* indicate logical relationships. *Meanwhile* (choice A) is a transition used to show time. *Furthermore* (choice C) is used when an additional point is being made. *Specifically* (choice D) is appropriate for introducing examples.

2. **The correct answer is C.** Progress reports keep supervisors up to date on the status of a project. An investigative report (choice A) is a report written when information is requested about a particular subject. A feasibility report (choice B) is a report that enables executives to determine whether an idea is possible and practical. A test report (choice D) is similar to a laboratory report but smaller and less formal.

3. **The correct answer is C.** White space is sometimes referred to as negative space because it is devoid of text or content. Margins (choice A), space between paragraphs (choice B), and gutters (choice D) are all examples of space in a document that does not contain content. Although white space might be present above or below a header, a header contains content, and thus, is not an example of white space.

4. **The correct answer is A.** Primary research is conducted by the technical writer and focuses solely on firsthand data, such as surveys, questionnaires, personally conducted interviews, etc. Choices B, C, and D are all true of secondary research.

5. **The correct answer is B.** Laboratory reports relay information gathered from an investigation or from laboratory testing. A technical writer could use the questions presented in choices A, C, and D to evaluate a laboratory report for completeness. Choice B asks the technical writer to consider whether the language is appropriate for the established purpose. It does not consider whether the writer has provided enough information for the document to achieve its purpose.

6. **The correct answer is A.** Question headings are useful in drawing readers into reading about a specific topic, but they are too informal for some documents, such as proposals. While statement headings (choice B) are more detailed than minor and major topic headings (choices C and D), these are all considered appropriate for proposals.

7. **The correct answer is B.** Audience adaptation refers to modifying the information in a technical document to make it appropriate for a specific audience. Abstracted information (choice A) and documented research (choice C) are elements of many technical documents, but neither refers to changing the language to suit the needs of readers. Choice D is incorrect because audience adaptation often occurs after a writer has analyzed the audience.

8. **The correct answer is C.** The primary purpose of a progress report is to provide an update on the completion status of a project. While progress reports do note changes to the project timeline when a team encounters a setback, choice A is not the best answer because that is not the primary purpose of the report. Choice B is more appropriate for a recommendation report while choice D is more appropriate for a short, informal proposal.

9. **The correct answer is A.** The sentence in choice A reflects correct parallel structure, which means that all elements in the sentence are alike in both form and function. Choice B is incorrect because "that suddenly" should be "who suddenly" to match "who either play." Choice C is incorrect because "a dangerous accident" should be replaced with the word *danger*. Choice D is incorrect because "breathing ability" should be replaced by the word *airways*.

10. **The correct answer is A.** Parallel structure requires words or phrases in sequence to exhibit the same form. In choice B, the phrase "nor was it" should be replaced by the word *nor*. In choices C and D, the last phrase in the sequence does not begin with a verb even though the first and second phrases do.

11. **The correct answer is C.** Possible *and* practical are the key ideas behind feasibility reports. An idea may be possible or promising, but whether it is practical determines if a company will go through with it.

12. **The correct answer is A.** Choice A is written concisely, is grammatically correct, and contains simple language that is not likely to confuse an audience who is unfamiliar with medical terminology. Choice B adds unnecessary words that do not help the reader understand the meaning of the sentence. Similarly, the transitional phrase "as well as" in choice D is wordy. Choice C uses medical jargon that might confuse general audiences.

13. **The correct answer is D.** In the original, the underlined content represents a misplaced modifier. A modifier is a phrase that provides more information about other words or phrases in a sentence. Modifiers must be placed as close as possible to the words or phrases that they modify. In this example, the modifier "following the experiment," modifies the uncontaminated sample and so it must be placed as close as possible to the phrase. In choices A, B, and C, the modifier is not placed in close proximity to the content it modifies.

14. **The correct answer is B.** The purpose of including the equipment and procedures in a laboratory report is so tests can be duplicated. This requires clearly written information about the equipment used and the procedures followed. Choices A, C, and D are incorrect because including information regarding equipment and procedures does not help a reader understand, explain, or recall the results.

15. **The correct answer is C.** There are two items that should be addressed. Choice A requires attention because it identifies a limitation of the potential solution. The technical writer should add a note indicating that the solution is not compatible with the LINUX operating system. Choice B contains a common grammatical mistake—a misplaced apostrophe. To indicate possession, the writer should use *its* instead of *it's*.

16. **The correct answer is B.** Choice B moves the information about methane closer to natural gas and places emphasis on the detail about coal beds. In choice C, the verb tense changes from present to past. The pronoun *it* in choice D is too far from natural gas, so the sentence is confusing.

17. **The correct answer is D.** The pronoun *its* needs to be close to *arena* for the sake of clarity. Choices A and B have the pronoun too far from *arena*. Choice C is unnecessarily wordy.

18. **The correct answer is D.** The stockholders did the accusing, so "by the stockholders" should be near *accused*. Choices A and C fail to do this. Choice B changes the entire meaning of the sentence.

19. **The correct answer is D.** Feasibility reports include a recommendations section, but laboratory reports do not.

20. **The correct answer is A.** A document containing highly technical language is most appropriate for an audience that consists of subject matter experts, who would not require extensive explanations of data or terms. Semi-technical language (choice B) is appropriate for an audience that consists of people with some technical knowledge but who are not quite as knowledgeable as experts. Indefinite (choice C) and subjective (choice D) language would not be appropriate for an audience with subject matter knowledge.

21. **The correct answer is D.** Writing in parallel structure, eliminating excess words, and sequencing information can enhance clarity in a document. Abstract terms (choice A) are not as clear as concrete ones. Transitions (choice B) improve clarity. Appendixes (choice C) do not necessarily improve clarity, and too many appendixes can clutter a document with irrelevant information.

22. **The correct answer is A.** When using columns in a document, orphans and widows should be avoided. An orphan is a word on a line by itself at the end of a column. A header (choice B) contains information such as title or page number. An outlier (choice C) is a statistical term. A widow (choice D) is a single line carried over to the top of a column.

23. **The correct answer is B.** Indirect patterns (i.e., presenting the main point last) are used in memos when presenting bad news, such as layoffs and salary cuts. Functional (choice A) and spatial (choice C) are not terms used for the structure of memos. Direct patterns (choice D) present the main point first, which would more than likely not be used to deliver bad news.

24. **The correct answer is C.** Flowcharts and schematic diagrams are appropriate for showing steps in a process or the relationships in a system. A representational diagram presents a realistic but simplified illustration of an item.

25. **The correct answer is D.** A document's glossary is usually placed after the bibliography and appendixes. A glossary is separate from the appendixes and would not be placed in an appendix as choice A indicates. Before the introduction (choice B) and in the front matter (choice C) are incorrect because the glossary is part of a document's back matter.

26. **The correct answer is D.** Gantt charts show how the phases of a project interrelate. Prose tables (choice A) organize verbal descriptions or instructions. Pictograms (choice B) are tables with representative symbols. Bar graphs (choice C) show comparisons.

27. **The correct answer is B.** The conclusion of a feasibility report interprets the findings of the study. The recommendation section is used to express the author's opinion, so choice A is incorrect. Options and costs are reviewed in the body of the report, so choices C and D are incorrect.

28. **The correct answer is D.** Numbering steps (choice C) in a process and using transitions (choice A) are both effective ways to enhance unity. Repeating key terms and major points (choice B) helps the reader keep the purpose of a document in mind. However, while explaining word origins is appropriate for some documents, it does not necessarily improve unity.

29. **The correct answer is B.** A pie graph is used to relate parts to a whole, so it is the best visual for showing what percentage of total sales each department generated. Tree charts (choice A) show how different aspects of an idea relate to one another. Line graphs (choice C) show how things change over time. An organizational chart (choice D) would show how each department in a group is connected.

30. **The correct answer is C.** A pictogram uses symbols instead of lines and bars to represent numerical amounts, so it is appropriate for nontechnical readers. Multiline graphs (choice A) and schematic diagrams (choice B) are less appropriate for nontechnical readers. A PERT chart (choice D) is similar to a Gantt chart and is used to schedule activities on a project.

31. **The correct answer is A.** Method is not an aspect of audience analysis. When performing an audience analysis, a technical writer should consider the attitude (choice B) readers have toward the subject matter as well as the needs (choice C) of the audience. Culture (choice D) is a consideration when an international audience will read a document.

32. **The correct answer is C.** Descriptive abstracts are included on the title page of documents. Closing summaries are inserted at the end of the body (choice A) and in the conclusion (choice B). The appendix (choice D) is not a typical location for summaries or abstracts.

33. **The correct answer is A.** The back matter of a long proposal includes the appendixes, bibliography, and glossary. Among other information, the body of a long proposal includes the cost analysis, rationale, and conclusion.

34. **The correct answer is B.** Changes over time are best illustrated with a line graph. Parts of a whole (choice A) are shown in a pie graph. Phases of a project (choice C) are shown in a Gantt chart. A sequence of events (choice D) is indicated in a flowchart.

35. **The correct answer is A.** Proposals differ from other technical writing because their purpose is to persuade readers. Product description (choice B) is an aspect of many different kinds of technical documents, not proposals. Likewise with audience analysis (choice C). Feasibility reports often compare options (choice D).

36. **The correct answer is B.** Each appendix should relate to one major item. Letters are used to identify each appendix, not numbers as choice A erroneously indicates. Choice C is incorrect because appendixes may be longer than one page. Appendixes should be arranged in the order they are mentioned in the text, not in order of importance as choice D indicates.

37. The correct answer is D. It is appropriate to include a persuasive pitch for a company, product, or service in the conclusion of a sales proposal. The conclusion should not introduce new statistics or other information not presented in the body (choice B). Neither a competitor's weaknesses (choice A) nor background information (choice C) is appropriate in a sales proposition.

38. The correct answer is C. Routine internal proposals are written for minor spending requests and permission to hire new employees. A formal internal proposal (choice A) is used when requesting large amounts of capital. Progress reports (choice B) describe how a project is going, and feasibility reports (choice D) discuss the practicality of an idea.

39. The correct answer is D. If chronological sequencing is employed, the correct order of sentences should be 3, 5, 1, 2, 4.

40. The correct answer is B. Both sentences provide descriptive content about what a spot contains, thus, they can be joined using a transition (such as *and*) that indicates addition. *However* (choice A) is a transition word that indicates contrast, which does not accurately describe the relationship between sentences 1 and 2 as they both describe the spot. *In sum* (choice C) would be used to summarize. *For example* (choice D) would be used to clarify a point using an example.

41. The correct answer is B. Headings serve to divide information in a document into logical pieces easily recognized by readers. Titles (choice A) provide readers with an indication of the subject of a document. Headers (choice D) and footers (choice C) are at the top and bottom of pages and usually indicate the page number and date of a document.

42. The correct answer is D. A status report, which is also called a progress report, summarizes the accomplishments related to one project during a given period. A periodic activity report summarizes general activities in a given period, which may relate to one employee or multiple departments in an organization.

43. **The correct answer is C.** The executive summary combines the main points of a proposal, and it is often the only section of a longer document ever read by an audience. Executive summaries follow the same sequence as the full document, but they are 10 percent of the length.

44. **The correct answer is A.** A printed source published by a university, professional organization, or museum is most likely reliable. Readability (choice B) helps the audience understand information but does not increase reliability. Soft evidence (choice C) is less reliable than hard evidence. The publication date (choice D) is important in determining whether a source is current, but it is less important when determining reliability.

45. **The correct answer is A.** The primary benefit of headings is to improve the readability of technical documents by helping readers easily locate information and recognize when topics have changed. Headings typically don't serve to clarify style and tone as choice B indicates. Although headings break up the monotony of paragraphs, choice C is not the best answer because they do not necessarily enhance the visual appeal of a document like graphs and charts do. Choice D is incorrect because headings are not so specific that they summarize main points.

46. **The correct answer is C.** A feasibility report should include a review of possible alternatives, specific recommendations, and an interpretation of options. It does not include procedures and instructions.

47. **The correct answer is D.** Even though grantmakers often have very specific and unique requirements, technical writers can expect to be asked to provide insight into project logistics. Like other types of proposals, grant proposals have a persuasive purpose; the technical writer must convince the grantmaker that the proposed project has value.

48. The correct answer is C. A drawing is effective in a report when a cutaway view of an internal mechanism is needed. Choice A calls for a photograph rather than a drawing. Choice B describes why symbols and icons are included in some reports. Maps are useful to illustrate locations and distances (choice D).

49. The correct answer is D. A paragraph describing the details of a solution is inappropriate for two reasons. First, a proposal presents persuasive content, and its cover letter should be similarly persuasive; thus, it should focus on benefits for the client, rather than technical specifications. The technical specifications appear in the body of the proposal. Second, a cover letter is intended to provide a concise statement of value for the client. A paragraph is too lengthy. Choice A represents a stronger design choice. Choice B is a cover letter element that contributes to a professional, courteous tone.

50. The correct answer is A. Choice A is written clearly, while choices B, C, and D are not. Choice B should be reworded to say "since you are so familiar." It is unclear in choice C whether *he* refers to the manager or the vice president. *All* and *not* in choice D create a confusing sentence.

51. The correct answer is C. Glossary terms are arranged alphabetically just like a dictionary. Terms are typically technical ones used in the field (technology, medicine, business, or science), so choice A is incorrect. Appendixes are listed in the order they appear, but not glossary terms, so choice B is incorrect. Items in a glossary should have clear and concise explanations, so choice D is incorrect.

52. The correct answer is D. Trained operators of construction and manufacturing equipment turn to operator manuals for reviewing safety information. Tutorials (choice A) and training manuals (choice C) are for unskilled users of a product or piece of equipment. Service manuals (choice B) are used by repair technicians.

53. The correct answer is B. Common goals, conflict management, and version control are all requirements of collaborative writing. A collaborative document is one that is produced by more than one person. Choice B is the only choice that indicates that the written document will be produced by more than one author.

54. The correct answer is C. The background section of a long proposal describes the problem that a proposal attempts to address. A general description of the product or service offered by a company is included in choice A. An itemization of cost estimates is provided in choice B. Site preparation (choice D) refers to any modifications that are necessary to a customer's facilities.

55. The correct answer is C. The purpose of any kind of technical communication is what readers should know, believe, or do after reading a document. Although an executive summary (choice A) may include the purpose of a document, it serves to present a concise version of the full document. The topic (choice B) is the subject matter of the document and does not necessarily indicate the author's purpose. The outline (choice D) helps organize information and does not specify an author's objective.

56. The correct answer is B. Executive summaries are slightly persuasive because the writer is trying to convince readers of what to think or do. Abstracts and summaries are typically read, not presented orally as choice A erroneously indicates. Only a closing summary is placed in the conclusion, so choice C is incorrect as well. Choice D is reflective of informative abstracts; executive summaries are 10 percent of the document's length.

57. The correct answer is C. Multiple sources improve the validity of information presented in a technical document. Statistical data (choice A) may be necessary in many documents, but if the data comes from only one source, it may not be reliable. The graphics and sponsorship of a website (choices B and D) do not improve the validity of information on the site.

58. **The correct answer is B.** The front matter of a long proposal includes the cover letter, title page, table of contents, and list of figures. The introduction is part of the body of a long proposal. While short proposals are divided into an introduction, body, and conclusion, the question is inquiring about long proposals.

59. **The correct answer is D.** Manuals provide guidelines and serve as a reference tool for users. Procedures specify what actions group members must take during certain situations, thus eliminating choice B as correct. Manuals are not persuasive, so choice A is incorrect. Results are not discussed in manuals, so choice C is incorrect.

60. **The correct answer is A.** Informative abstracts are written for general audiences that consist of readers with different levels of knowledge. Informative abstracts should not be written only for experts and academics, so choices B and C are incorrect. Many readers of abstracts do not have the time to read an entire report, but that does not mean they have no interest at all, thus eliminating choice D.

Like what you see? Get unlimited access to Peterson's full catalog of DSST practice tests, instructional videos, flashcards, and more for **75% off the first month!** Go to **www.petersons.com/testprep/dsst** and use coupon code **DSST2020** at checkout. Offer expires July 1, 2021.